INITIATION INTO PHILOSOPHY

INITIATION INTO PHILOSOPHY

By

EMILE FAGUET

GYAN

Published by

GYAN

Gyan Publishing House
5, Ansari Road
Daryaganj, New Delhi-110002
Phone: 011-47034999, 9811692060
E-mail: books@gyanbooks.com

Distribution Network
gyanbooks.com
India, USA, Canada, UK, Australia, France

ISBN : 978-81-212-6422-8 (PB)
First Published, 1912

2nd Impression 2022

Printed at: Gyan Press, Delhi.

INITIATION INTO PHILOSOPHY
Author: EMILE FAGUET

INITIATION INTO PHILOSO

BY

EMILE FAGUET

1912

INITIATION

This volume, as indicated by the title, is designed to show the way to the beginner, to satisfy and more especially to excite his initial curiosity. It affords an adequate idea of the march of facts and of ideas. The reader is led, somewhat rapidly, from the remote origins to the most recent efforts of the human mind.

It should be a convenient repertory to which the mind may revert in order to see broadly the general opinion of an epoch—and what connected it with those that followed or preceded it. It aims above all at being *a frame* in which can conveniently be inscribed, in the course of further studies, new conceptions more detailed and more thoroughly examined.

It will have fulfilled its design should it incite to research and meditation, and if it prepares for them correctly.

E. Faguet.

TABLE OF CONTENTS.

PART I.

ANTIQUITY.

CHAPTER I.
BEFORE SOCRATES.

Philosophical Interpreters of the Universe, of the Creation and Constitution of the World - - - - - - 9

CHAPTER II.
THE SOPHISTS.

Logicians and Professors of Logic and of the Analysis of Ideas and of Discussion - - - - - - 13

CHAPTER III.
SOCRATES.

Philosophy entirely reduced to Morality, and Morality considered as the end of all Intellectual Activity - 18

CHAPTER IV.
PLATO.

Plato, like Socrates, is pre-eminently a Moralist, but he reverts to General Consideration of the Universe, and he deals with Politics and Legislation - - - 25

CONTENTS

CHAPTER V.

ARISTOTLE.

A Man of Encyclopædic Learning; as Philosopher more especially Moralist and Logician - - - - 29

CHAPTER VI.

VARIOUS SCHOOLS.

The Development in Various Schools of the General Ideas of Socrates, Plato and Aristotle - - - 34

CHAPTER VII.

EPICUREANISM.

Epicureanism believes that the Duty of Man is to seek Happiness, and that Happiness consists in Wisdom - 39

CHAPTER VIII.

STOICISM.

The Passions are Diseases which can and must be extirpated - - - - - - - - 42

CHAPTER IX.

ECLECTICS AND SCEPTICS.

Philosophers who wished to belong to no School. Philosophers who decried all Schools and all Doctrines - - - - - - - 46

CHAPTER X.

NEOPLATONISM.

Reversion to Metaphysics. Imaginative Metaphysicians after the manner of Plato, but in excess - - 50

CHAPTER XI.

CHRISTIANITY.

Philosophic Ideas which Christianity welcomed, adopted or created; how it must give a fresh Aspect to all Philosophy, even that foreign to itself - - - 64

PART II.

IN THE MIDDLE AGES.

CHAPTER I.

FROM THE FIFTH CENTURY TO THE THIRTEENTH.

Philosophy is only an Interpreter of Dogma. When it is declared contrary to Dogma by the Authority of Religion, it is a Heresy. Orthodox and heterodox Interpretations. Some Independent Philosophers - 77

CHAPTER II.

THE THIRTEENTH CENTURY.

Influence of Aristotle. His Adoption by the Church. Religious Philosophy of St. Thomas Aquinas - 86

CHAPTER III.

THE FOURTEENTH AND FIFTEENTH CENTURIES.

Decadence of Scholasticism. Forebodings of the Coming Era. Great Moralists. The Kabbala. Sorcery - 91

CHAPTER IV.

THE SIXTEENTH CENTURY.

It is fairly accurate to consider that from the Point of View of Philosophy, the Middle Ages lasted until Descartes. Free-thinkers more or less disguised. Partisans of Reason apart from Faith, Observation and Experiment - - - - - 104

CONTENTS

PART III.

MODERN TIMES.

CHAPTER I.

THE SEVENTEENTH CENTURY.

Descartes. Cartesianism - - - - - - - 124

CHAPTER II.

CARTESIANS.

All the Seventeenth Century was under the Influence of Descartes. Port-Royal, Bossuet, Fénelon. Malebranche, Spinoza, Leibnitz - - - - - - 141

CHAPTER III.

THE ENGLISH PHILOSOPHERS OF THE SEVENTEENTH CENTURY.

Locke: His Ideas on Human Liberty, Morality, General Politics, and Religious Politics - - - 146

CHAPTER IV.

THE ENGLISH PHILOSOPHERS OF THE EIGHTEENTH CENTURY.

Berkeley: A highly Idealist Philosophy which regarded Matter as non-existent. David Hume: Sceptical Philosophy. The Scottish School: Philosophy of Common Sense - - - - - - - 152

CHAPTER V.

THE FRENCH PHILOSOPHERS OF THE EIGHTEENTH CENTURY.

Voltaire a Disciple of Locke. Rousseau a Free-thinking Christian, but deeply imbued with Religious Sentiments. Diderot a capricious Materialist. D'Holbach and Helvetius avowed Materialists. Condillac a Philosopher of Sensations - - - - - - 156

CHAPTER VI.

KANT.

Kant reconstructed all Philosophy by resting it on Morality - - - - - - - - - - 167

CHAPTER VII.

THE NINETEENTH CENTURY: GERMANY.

The great Reconstructors of the World, analogous to the first Philosophers of Antiquity. Great General Systems, Fichte, Schelling, Hegel, &c. - - - 181

CHAPTER VIII.

THE NINETEENTH CENTURY: ENGLAND.

The Doctrines of Evolution and of Transformism: Lamarck (French), Darwin, Spencer - - - 184

CHAPTER IX.

THE NINETEENTH CENTURY: FRANCE.

The Eclectic School: Victor Cousin. The Positivist School: Auguste Comte. The Kantist School: Renouvier. Independent and Complex Positivists: Taine, Renan - - - - - - - - - 194

INDEX - - - - - - - - 197

Part I.

ANTIQUITY.

CHAPTER I.

BEFORE SOCRATES.

Philosophical Interpreters of the Universe, of the Creation and Constitution of the World.

PHILOSOPHY.—The aim of philosophy is to seek the explanation of all things: the quest is for the first *causes* of everything, and also *how* all things are and finally *why*, with what design, with a view to what, things are. That is why, taking "principle" in all the senses of the word, it has been called the science of first principles.

Philosophy has always existed. Religions—all religions—are philosophies. They are indeed the most complete. But, apart from religions, men have sought the causes and principles of everything and endeavoured to acquire general ideas. These researches apart from religious dogmas in pagan antiquity are the only ones with which we are here to be concerned.

THE IONIAN SCHOOL: THALES.—The Ionian School is the most ancient school of philosophy known. It dates back to the seventh century before Christ. Thales of Miletus, a natural philosopher and astronomer, as we should describe him, believed matter—namely, that of which all things and all beings are made—to be in perpetual transformation, and that these transformations are produced by powerful beings attached to every portion of matter. These powerful beings were gods. Everything, therefore, was full of gods. His philosophy was a mythology. He also thought that the essential element of matter was water, and that it was water, under the influence of the gods, which transformed itself into earth, air, and fire, whilst from water, earth, air and fire came everything that is in nature.

ANAXIMANDER: HERACLITUS.—Anaximander of Miletus, an astronomer also, and a geographer, believed that the principle of all things is *indeterminate*—a kind of chaos wherein nothing has form or shape; that from chaos come things and beings, and that they return thither in order to emerge again. One of his particular theories was that fish were the most ancient of animals, and that all animals had issued from them through successive transformations. This theory was revived for a while about fifty years ago.

Heraclitus of Ephesus (very obscure, and with this epithet attached permanently to his name) saw all things as a perpetual growth—in an indefinite state of becoming. Nothing is; all things grow and are destined to eternal growth. Behind them, nevertheless, there is an eternal master who does not change. It is our duty to resemble him as much as we can; that is to say, as much as an ape can resemble a man. Calmness is imperative: to be as motionless as transient beings can. The popular legend runs that Heraclitus "always wept"; what is known of him only tends to prove that he was grave, and did not favour emotionalism.

ANAXAGORAS: EMPEDOCLES.—Anaxagoras of Clazomenæ, above all else a natural philosopher, settled at Athens about 470 B.C.; was the master and friend of Pericles; was on the point of being put to death, as Socrates was later on, for the crime of indifference towards the religion of the Athenians, and had to take refuge at Lampsacus, where he died. Like Anaximander, he believed that everything emerged from something indeterminate and confused; but he added that what caused the emergence from that state was the organising intelligence, the Mind, just as in man it is the intelligence which draws thought from cerebral undulations, and forms a clear idea out of a confused idea. Anaxagoras exerted an almost incomparable influence over Greek philosophy of the classical times.

Empedocles of Agrigentum, a sort of magician

and high-priest, almost a deity, whose life and death are but little known, appears to have possessed an encyclopædic brain. From him is derived the doctrine of the four elements, for whereas the philosophers who preceded him gave as the sole source of things—some water, others air, others fire, others the earth, he regarded them all four equally as the primal elements of everything. He believed that the world is swayed by two contrary forces—love and hate, the one desiring eternally to unite, the other eternally to disintegrate. Amid this struggle goes on a movement of organization, incessantly retarded by hate, perpetually facilitated by love; and from this movement have issued—first, vegetation, then the lower animals, then the higher animals, then men. In Empedocles can be found either evident traces of the religion of Zoroaster of Persia (the perpetual antagonism of two great gods, that of good and that of evil), or else a curious coincidence with this doctrine, which will appear again later among the Manicheans.

Pythagoras.—Pythagoras appears to have been born about B.C. 500 on the Isle of Elea, to have travelled much and to have finally settled in Greater Greece (southern Italy). Pythagoras, like Empedocles, was a sort of magician or god. His doctrine was a religion, the respect with which he was surrounded was a cult, the observances he imposed on his family and on his disciples were rites. What he taught was that the true realities, which do not change, were numbers. The fundamental and supreme reality is *one*; the being who is one is God; from this number, which is one, are derived all the other numbers which are the foundation of beings, their inward cause, their essence; we are all more or less perfect numbers; each created thing is a more or less perfect number. The world, governed thus by combinations of numbers, has always existed and will always exist. It develops itself, however, according to a numerical series of which we do not possess the key, but which we can guess. As for human destiny it is this: we have been animated beings, human or animal; according as we have lived well or ill we shall be reincarnated either as superior men or as animals more or less inferior. This is the doctrine of *metempsychosis*, which had many adherents in ancient days, and also in a more or less fanciful fashion in modern times.

To Pythagoras have been attributed a certain number of maxims which are called the *Golden Verses*.

XENOPHANES: PARMENIDES. — Xenophanes of Colophon is also a "unitarian." He only accepts one God, and of all the ancient philosophers appears to be the most opposed to mythology, to belief in a multiplicity of gods resembling men, a doctrine which he despises as being immoral. There is one God, eternal, immutable, immovable, who has no need to transfer Himself from one locality to another, who is *without place*, and who governs all things by His thought alone.

Advancing further, Parmenides told himself that if He alone really exists who is one and eternal and unchangeable, all else is not only inferior to Him, but is only a *semblance*, and that mankind, earth, sky, plants, and animals, are only a vast illusion—phantoms, a mirage, which would disappear, which would no longer exist, and *would never have existed* if we could perceive the Self-existent.

ZENO : DEMOCRITUS.—Zeno of Elea, who must be mentioned more especially because he was the master of that Gorgias of whom Socrates was the adversary, was pre-eminently a subtle dialectician in whom the sophist already made his appearance, and who embarrassed the Athenians by captious arguments, at the bottom of which always could be found this fundamental principle : apart from the Eternal Being all is only semblance ; apart from Him who is all, all is nothing.

Democritus of Abdera, disciple of Leucippus

of Abdera (about whom nothing is known), is the inventor of the theory of atoms. Matter is composed of an infinite number of tiny indivisible bodies which are called atoms ; these atoms from all eternity, or at least since the commencement of matter, have been endued with certain movements by which they attach themselves to one another, and agglomerate or separate, and thence is caused the formation of all things, and the destruction, which is only the disintegration, of all things. The soul itself is only an aggregation of specially tenuous and subtle atoms. It is probable that when a certain number of these atoms quit the body, sleep ensues; that when nearly all depart, it causes the appearance of death (lethargy, catalepsy); that when they all depart, death occurs. We are brought into relation with the external world by the advent in us of extremely subtle atoms—reflections of things, semblances of things—which enter and mingle with the constituent atoms of our souls. There is nothing in our intelligence which has not been brought there by our senses, and our intelligence is only the combination of the atoms composing our souls with the atoms that external matter sends, so to speak, into our souls. The doctrines of Democritus will be found again in those of Epicurus and Lucretius.

CHAPTER II.

THE SOPHISTS.

Logicians and Professors of Logic, and of the Analysis of Ideas, and of Discussion.

Doctrines of the Sophists.—The Sophists descend from Parmenides and Zeno of Elea; Gorgias was the disciple of the latter. By dint of thinking that all is semblance save the Supreme Being, who alone is real, it is very easy to arrive at belief in all being semblance, including that Being; or at least what is almost tantamount, that all is semblance inclusive of any idea we can possibly conceive of the Supreme Being. To believe nothing, and to demonstrate that there is no reason to believe in anything, is the cardinal principle of all the Sophists. Then, it may be suggested, there is nothing for it but to be silent. No, there is the cultivation of one's mind (the only thing of the existence of which we are sure), so as to give it ability, readiness and strength. With what object? To become a dexterous thinker, which in itself is a fine thing; to be also a man of consideration, listened to in one's city, and to arrive at its government.

The Sophists accordingly gave lessons, especially in psychology, dialectics and eloquence. They further taught philosophy, but in order to demonstrate that all philosophy is false; and as Pascal observed later that to ridicule philosophy is truly philosophical. They seem to have been extremely intellectual, very learned, and most serious despite their scepticism, and to have rendered Greece the very great service of making a penetrating analysis—the first recorded—of our faculty of knowledge and of the limitations, real, possible or probable, of that faculty.

PROTAGORAS : GORGIAS : PRODICUS.—They were very numerous, the taste for their art, which might be called philosophical criticism, being widespread in Attica. It may be believed, as Plato maintains, that some were of very mediocre capacity, and this is natural; but there were also some who clearly were eminent authorities. The most illustrious were Protagoras, Gorgias, and Prodicus of Ceos. Protagoras seems to have been the most philosophical of them all, Gorgias the best orator and the chief professor of rhetoric, Prodicus the most eminent moralist and poet. Protagoras rejected all metaphysics—that is, all investigation of first causes and of the universe—and reduced all philosophy to the science of self-control with a view to happiness, and control of others with a view to their happiness. Like Anaxagoras, he was banished from the city under the charge of impiety, and his books were publicly burnt.

Gorgias appears to have maintained the same ideas with more moderation and also with less profundity. He claimed, above all, to be able to make a good orator. According to Plato, it was he whom Socrates most persistently made the butt of his sarcasms.

Prodicus, whom Plato himself esteemed, appears to have been principally preoccupied with the moral problem. He was the author of the famous apologue which represented Hercules having to choose between two paths, the one being that of virtue, the other of pleasure. Like Socrates later on, he too was subject to the terrible accusation of impiety, and underwent capital punishment. The Sophists furnish the most important epoch in the history of ancient philosophy; until their advent the philosophic systems were great poems on the total of all things, known and unknown. The Sophists opposed these ambitious and precipitate generalizations, in which imagination had the larger share, and their discovery was to bring philosophy back to its true starting point by affirming that the first thing to do, and that before all else, was to know our own mind and its mechanism. Their error possibly was, while saying that it was the first thing to do, too often to affirm that it was the only thing to do; still the fact remains that they were perfectly accurate in their assurance that it was primary.

CHAPTER III.

SOCRATES.

Philosophy entirely reduced to Morality, and Morality considered as the End of all Intellectual Activity.

THE PHILOSOPHY OF SOCRATES.—Of Socrates nothing is known except that he was born at Athens, that he held many public discussions with all and sundry in the streets of Athens, and that he died under the Thirty Tyrants. Of his ideas we know nothing, because he wrote nothing, and because his disciples were far too intelligent; in consequence of which it is impossible to know if what they said was thought by him, had really been his ideas or theirs. What seems certain is that neither Aristophanes nor the judges at the trial of Socrates were completely deceived in considering him a Sophist; for he proceeded from them. It is true he proceeded from them by reaction, because evidently their universal scepticism had terrified him; but nevertheless he was their direct outcome, for like them he was extremely mistrustful of the old vast systems of philosophy, and to those men who pretended to know everything, he opposed a phrase which is probably authentic: "I know that I know nothing" ; for, like the Sophists, he wished to recall philosophy to earth from heaven, namely from metaphysics to the study of man, and nothing else ; for, like the Sophists, he confined and limited the field with a kind of severe and imperious modesty which was none the less contemptuous of the audacious ; for, finally, like the Sophists, but in this highly analogous to many philosophers preceding the Sophists, he had but a very moderate and mitigated respect for the religion of his fellow-citizens.

According to what we know of Socrates from Xenophon, unquestionably the least imaginative of his disciples, Socrates, like the Sophists, reduced philosophy to the study of man ; but his great and incomparable originality lay in the fact that whereas the Sophists wished man to study himself in order to be happy, Socrates wished him to study himself in order to be moral, honest and just, without any regard to happiness. For Socrates everything had to tend towards morality, to contribute to it, and to be subordinated to it as the goal and as the final aim. He applied himself unceasingly, relates Xenophon, to examine and to determine what is good and evil, just and unjust, wise and foolish, brave and cowardly, etc. He incessantly applied himself, relates Aristotle—and therein he was as much a true professor of rhetoric as of morality—thoroughly to define and carefully to specify the meaning of words in order not to be put off with vague terms which are illusions of thought, and in order to discipline his mind rigorously so as to make it an organ for the ascertainment of truth.

His Method.—He had dialectical methods, "the art of conferring," as Montaigne called it, more or less happy, which he had probably borrowed from the Sophists, that contributed to cause him to be considered one of them, and exercised a wide vogue long after him. He "delivered men's minds," as he himself said—that is, he believed, or affected to believe, that the verities are in a latent state in all minds, and that it only needed patience, dexterity and skilful investigation to bring them to light. Elsewhere, he *interrogated* in a captious fashion in order to set the interlocutor in contradiction to himself and to make him confess that he had said what he had not thought he had said, agreed to what he had not believed he had agreed to; and he triumphed maliciously over such confusions. In short, he seems to have been a witty and teasing Franklin, and to have taught true wisdom by laughing at everyone. Folk never like to be ridiculed, and no doubt the recollection of these ironies had much to do with the iniquitous judgment which condemned him, and which he seems to have challenged up to the last.

His Influence.—His influence was infinite. It is from him that morality became the end itself, the last and supreme end of all philosophy—the reason of philosophy; and, as was observed by Nietzsche, the Circe of philosophers, who enchants them, who dictates to them beforehand, or who modifies their systems in advance by terrifying them as to what their systems may contain irreverent towards itself or dangerous in relation to it. From Socrates to Kant and thence onward, morality has been the Circe of philosophers and morality is, as it were, the spiritual daughter of Socrates. On the other hand, his influence was terrible for the religion of antiquity because it directed the mind towards the idea that morality is the sole object worthy of knowledge, and that the ancient religions were immoral, or of such a dubious morality as to deserve the desertion and scorn of honest men. Christianity fought paganism with the arguments of the disciples of Socrates—with Socratic arguments; modern philosophies and creeds are all impregnated with Socraticism. When it was observed that the Sophists form the most important epoch in the history of ancient philosophy, it was because they taught Socrates to seek a philosophy which was entirely human and preoccupied solely with the happiness of man. This led a great mind, and in his track other very great minds, to direct all philosophy, and even all human science, towards the investigation of goodness, goodness being regarded as the condition of happiness.

CHAPTER IV.

PLATO.

Plato, like Socrates, is pre-eminently a Moralist, but he reverts to general consideration of the Universe, and deals with Politics and Legislation.

PLATO A DISCIPLE OF SOCRATES.—Plato, like Xenophon, was a pupil of Socrates, but Xenophon only wanted to be the clerk of Socrates; and Plato, as an enthusiastic disciple, was at the same time very faithful and very unfaithful to Socrates. He was a faithful disciple to Socrates in never failing to place morality in the foremost rank of all philosophical considerations: in that he never varied. He was an unfaithful disciple to Socrates in that, imaginative and an admirable poet, he bore back philosophy from earth to heaven; he did not forbid himself—quite the contrary—to pile up great systems about all things and to envelop the universe in his vast and daring conceptions. He invincibly established morality, the science of virtue, as the final goal of human knowledge, in his brilliant and charming *Socratic Dialogues*: he formed great systems in all the works in which he introduces himself as speaking in his own name. He was very learned, and acquainted with everything that had been written by all the philosophers before Socrates, particularly Heraclitus, Pythagoras, Parmenides and Anaxagoras. He reconsidered all their teaching, and he himself brought to consideration a force and a wealth of mind such as appear to have had no parallel in the world.

THE "IDEAS."—Seeking, in his turn, what are the first causes of all and what is eternally real behind the simulations of this transient world, he believed in a single God, as had many before him; but in the bosom of this God, so to speak, he placed, he seemed to see, *Ideas*, that is to say, eternal types of all things which in this world are variable, transient and perishable. What he effected by such novel, original, and powerful imagination is clear. He replaced the Olympus of the populace by a spiritual Olympus; the material mythology by an idealistic mythology; polytheism by polyideism, if it may be so expressed—the gods by types. Behind every phenomenon, stream, forest, mountain, the Greeks perceived a deity, a material being like themselves, more powerful than themselves. Behind every phenomenon, behind every thought as well, every feeling, every institution—behind *everything, no matter what it be*, Plato perceived an idea, immortal, eternal, indestructible and incorruptible, which existed in the bosom of the Eternal, and of which all that comes under our observation is only the vacillating and troubled reflection, and which supports, animates and for a time preserves everything that we can perceive. Hence, all philosophy consists in having some knowledge of these Ideas. How is it possible to attain such knowledge? By raising the mind from the particular to the general; by distinguishing in each thing what is its permanent foundation, what it contains that is least changing, least variable, least circumstantial. For example, a man is a very complex being; he has countless feelings, countless diversified ideas, countless methods of conduct and existence. What is his permanent foundation? It is his conscience, which does not vary, undergoes no transformation, always obstinately repeats the same thing; the foundation of man, the eternal idea of which every man on earth is here the reflection, is the consciousness of good; man is an incarnation on earth of that part of God which is the will for good; according as he diverges from or approaches more nearly to this will, is he less or more man.

THE PLATONIC DIALECTIC AND MORALITY.—This method of raising oneself to the ideas is what Plato termed dialectic, that is to say, the art of discernment. Dialectic differentiates between the fundamental and the superficial, the permanent and the transient, the indestructible and the destructible. This is the supreme philosophic method which contains all the others and to which all the others are reduced. Upon this metaphysic and by the aid of this dialectic, Plato constructed an extremely pure system of morality which was simply an *Imitation of God* (as, later on, came the Imitation of Jesus Christ). The whole duty of man was to be as like God as he could. In God exist the ideas of truth, goodness, beauty, greatness, power, etc; man ought to aim at relatively realising those ideas which God absolutely realises. God is just, or justice lies in the bosom of God, which is the same thing; man cannot be the just one, but he can be a just man, and there is the whole matter; for justice comprises everything, or, to express it differently, is the characteristic common to all which is valuable. Justice is goodness, justice is beautiful, justice is true; justice is great, because it reduces all particular cases to one general principle; justice is powerful, being the force which maintains, opposed to the force which destroys; justice is eternal and invariable. To be just in all the meanings of the word is the duty of man and his proper goal.

THE IMMORTALITY OF THE SOUL.—Plato shows marked reserve as to the immortality of the soul and as to rewards and penalties beyond the grave. He is neither in opposition nor formally favourable. We feel that he wishes to believe in it rather than that he is sure about it. He says that "it is a fine wager to make;" which means that even should we lose, it is better to believe in this possible gain than to disbelieve. Further, it is legitimate to conclude—both from certain passages in the *Laws* and from the beautiful theory of Plato on the punishment which is an expiation, and on the expiation which is medicinal to the soul and consequently highly desirable—that Plato often inclined strongly towards the doctrine of posthumous penalties and rewards, which presupposes the immortality of the soul.

Platonic Love.—Platonic love, about which there has been so much talk and on which, consequently, we must say a word, at least to define it, is one of the applications of his moral system. As in the case of all other things, the idea of love is in God. There it exists in absolute purity, without any mixture of the idea of pleasure, since pleasure is essentially ephemeral and perishable. Love in God consists simply in the impassioned contemplation of beauty (physical and moral); we shall resemble God if we love beauty precisely in this way, without excitement or agitation of the senses.

Politics.—One of the originalities in Plato is that he busies himself with politics, that is, that he has made politics a part of philosophy, which had been barely thought of before him (I say *barely*, because Pythagoras was a legislator), and has ever since been taken into consideration. Plato is aristocratic, no doubt because his thought is generally such, independently of circumstances, also perhaps because he attributed the great misfortunes of his country which he witnessed to the Athenian democracy ; then yet again, perhaps, because that Athenian democracy had been violently hostile and sometimes cruel to philosophers, and more especially to his own master. According to Plato, just as man has three souls, or if it be preferred, three centres of activity, which govern him—intelligence in the head, courage in the heart, and appetite in the bowels—even so the city is composed of three classes : wise and learned men at the top, the warriors below, and the artisans and slaves lower still. The wise men will govern : accordingly the nations will never be happy save when philosophers are kings, or when kings are philosophers. The warriors will fight to defend the city, never as aggressors. They will form a caste—poor, stern to itself, and redoubtable. They will have no individual possessions ; everything will be in common, houses, furniture, weapons, wives even, and children. The people, finally, living in strict equality, either by equal partition of land, or on land cultivated in common, will be strictly maintained in probity, honesty, austerity, morality, sobriety and submissiveness. All arts, except military music and war dances, will be eliminated from the city. She needs neither poets nor painters nor yet musicians, who corrupt morals by softening them, and by making all feel the secret pang of voluptuousness. All theories, whether aristocratic or tending more or less to communism, are derived from the politics of Plato either by being evolved from them or by harking back to them.

The Master of the Idealistic Philosophy.—Plato is for all thinkers, even for his opponents, the greatest name in human philosophy. He is the supreme authority of the idealistic philosophy—that is, of all philosophy which believes that ideas govern the world, and that the world is progressing towards a perfection which is somewhere and which directs and attracts it. For those even who are not of his school, Plato is the most prodigious of all the thinkers who have united psychological wisdom, dialectical strength, the power of abstraction and creative imagination, which last in him attains to the marvellous.

CHAPTER V.

ARISTOTLE.

A Man of Encyclopædic Learning; as Philosopher, more especially Moralist and Logician.

ARISTOTLE, PUPIL OF PLATO.—Aristotle of Stagira was a pupil of Plato, and he remembered it, as the best pupils do as a rule, in order to oppose him. For some years he was tutor to Alexander, son of Philip, the future Alexander the Great. He taught long at Athens. After the death of Alexander, being the target in his turn of the eternal accusation of impiety, he was forced to retire to Chalcis, where he died. Aristotle is, before all else, a learned man. He desired to embrace the whole of the knowledge of his time, which was then possible by dint of prodigious effort, and he succeeded. His works, countless in number, are the record of his knowledge. They are the *summa* of all the sciences of his epoch. Here we have only to occupy ourselves with his more specially philosophical ideas. To Aristotle, as to Plato, but more precisely, man is composed of soul and body. The body is composed of organs, a well-made piece of mechanism; the soul is its final purpose; the body, so to speak, results in the soul, but, in turn, the soul acts on the body, and is in it not its end but its means of acting upon things, and the whole forms a full and continuous harmony. The faculties of the soul are its divers aspects, and its divers methods of acting; for the soul is one and indivisible. Reason is the soul considered as being able to conceive what is most general, and in consequence it forms within us an intermediary between ourselves and God. God is unique; He is eternal; from all eternity He has given motion to matter. He is purely spiritual, but all is material save Him, and He has not, as Plato would have it, *ideas*—immaterial living personifications—residing in His bosom. Here may be perceived, in a certain sense, progress, from Plato to Aristotle, towards monotheism; the Olympus of ideas in Plato was still a polytheism, a spiritual polytheism certainly, yet none the less a polytheism; there is no longer any polytheism at all in Aristotle.

His Theories of Morals and Politics.—The moral system of Aristotle sometimes approaches that of Plato, as when he deems that the supreme happiness is the supreme good, and that the supreme good is the contemplation of thought by thought—thought being self-sufficing; which is approximately the imitation of God which Plato recommended. Sometimes, on the contrary, it is very practical and almost mediocre, as when he makes it consist of a mean between the extremes, a just measure, a certain tact, art rather than science and practical science rather than conscience, which will know how to distinguish which are the practices suitable for an honest and a well-born man. It is only just to add that in detail and when after all deductions he describes the just man, he invites us to contemplate virtues which if not sublime are none the less remarkably lofty.

His very confused political philosophy (the volume containing it, according to all appearance, having been composed, after his death, of passages and fragments and different portions of his lectures) is specially a review of the divergent political constitutions which existed throughout the Greek world. The tendencies, for there are no conclusions, are still very aristocratic, but less radically aristocratic than those of Plato.

The authority of Aristotle.—Aristotle, by reason of his universality, also because he is more clear than his master, and again because he dogmatises—not always, but most often—instead of discussing and collating, had throughout both antiquity and the middle ages an authority greater than that of Plato, an authority which became (except on matters of faith) despotic and well-nigh sacrosanct. Since the sixteenth century he has been relegated to his due rank—one which is still very distinguished, and he has been regarded as among the geniuses of the widest range, if not of the greatest power, that have appeared among men ; even now he is very far from having lost his importance. For some he is a transition between the Greek genius—extremely subtle, but always poetic and always somewhat oriental—and the Roman genius : more positive, more bald, more practical, more attached to reality and to pure science.

CHAPTER VI.

VARIOUS SCHOOLS.

The Development in Various Schools of the General Ideas of Socrates, Plato, and Aristotle.

THE SCHOOL OF PLATO. THEOPHRASTUS.—The school of Plato (not regarding Aristotle as belonging entirely to that school) was continued by Speusippus, Polemo, Xenocrates, Crates and Crantor. Owing to a retrograde movement, widely different from that of Aristotle, it dabbled in the Pythagorean ideas, with which Plato was acquainted and which he often appreciated, but not blindly, and to which he never confined himself.

The most brilliant pupil of Aristotle was Theophrastus, naturalist, botanist and moralist. His great claim to fame among posterity, which knows nothing of him but this, is the small volume of *Characters*, which served as a model for La Bruyère, and before him to the comic poets of antiquity, and which is full of wit and flavour, and—to make use of a modern word exactly applicable to this ancient work—" humour."

SCHOOLS OF MEGARA AND OF ELIS.—We may just mention the very celebrated schools which, owing to lack of texts, are unknown to us—that of Megara, which was called the Eristic or "wrangling" school, so marked was its predilection for polemics; and that of Elis, which appears to have been well versed in the sophistic methods of Zeno of Elea and of Gorgias.

THE CYNIC SCHOOL. ANTISTHENES: DIOGENES. —Much more important is the Cynic school, because a school, which was nothing less than Stoicism itself, emanated or appeared to emanate from it. As often happens, the vague commencements of Stoicism bore a close resemblance to its end. The Stoics of the last centuries of antiquity were a sort of mendicant friars, ill-clothed, ill-fed, of neglected appearance, despising all the comforts of life; the Cynics at the time of Alexander were much the same, professing that happiness is the possession of all good things, and that the only way to possess all things is to know how to do without them. It was Antisthenes who founded this school, or rather this order. He had been the pupil of Socrates, and there can be no doubt that his sole idea was to imitate Socrates by exaggeration. Socrates had been poor, had scorned wealth, had derided pleasure and poured contempt on science. The cult of poverty, the contempt for pleasures, for honours, for riches, and the perfect conviction that any knowledge is perfectly useless to man—that is all the teaching of Antisthenes. That can lead far, at least in systematic minds. If all is contemptible except individual virtue, it is reversion to savage and solitary existence which is preached: there is no more civilization or society or patriotism. Antisthenes in these ideas was surpassed by his disciples and successors; they were cosmopolitans and anarchists. The most illustrious of this school —illustrious especially through his eccentricity— was Diogenes, who rolled on the ramparts of Corinth the tub which served him as a house, lighted his lantern in broad daylight on the pretext of "searching for a man," called himself a citizen of the world, was accused of being banished from Sinope by his fellow-countrymen and replied: "It was I who condemned them to remain," and said to Alexander, who asked him what he could do for him, "Get out of my sunshine, you are putting me in the shade."

Crates: Menippus: Aristippus.—Crates of Thebes is also mentioned, less insolent and better-mannered, yet also a despiser of the goods of this world; and Menippus, the maker of satires, whom Lucian, much later, made the most diverting interlocutor of his amusing dialogues. In an opposite direction, at the same epoch, Aristippus, a pupil of Socrates, like Antisthenes, founded the school of pleasure, and maintained that the sole search worthy of man was that of happiness, and that it was his duty to make himself happy; that in consequence, it having been sufficiently proved and being even self-evident, that happiness cannot come to us from without, but must be sought within ourselves, it is necessary to study to know ourselves thoroughly (and this was from Socrates) in order to decide what are the states of the mind which give us a durable, substantial and, if possible, a permanent happiness. Now the seeker and the finder of substantial happiness is wisdom, or rather, there is no other wisdom than the art of distinguishing between pleasures and choosing, with a very refined discrimination, those which are genuine. Wisdom further consists in dominating misfortunes by the mastery of self so as not to be affected by them, and in dominating also pleasures even whilst enjoying them, so that they may not obtain dominion over us; "possessing without being possessed" was one of his mottoes which Horace thus translated: "I strive to subject things to myself, not myself to things." This eminently practical wisdom, which is only a highly-developed egoism, is that of Horace and Montaigne, and was expressed by Voltaire in verses that were sometimes felicitous.

The School of Cyrene.—Aristippus had for successor in the direction of his school, first his daughter Arete, then his grandson. The

Aristippists or Cyrenaics (the school being established in Cyrene), frankly despised the gods, regarding them as inventions to frighten women and little children. One of them, Euhemerus, invented the theory, which in part is false and in part accurate, that the gods are simply heroes, kings, great men deified after their death by the gratitude or terror of the populace. As often happens, philosophic theories being essentially plastic and taking the form of the temperament which receives them, a certain Cyrenaic (Hegesias), enunciated the doctrine that the supreme happiness of man was suicide. In fact, if the object of man is happiness, since life affords far fewer joys than sorrows, the philosophy of happiness is to get rid of life, and the sole wisdom lies in suicide. It does not appear that Hegesias gave the only proof of sincere belief in this doctrine which can be given by anyone professing it.

CHAPTER VII.

EPICUREANISM.

Epicureanism believes that the duty of Man is to seek Happiness, and that Happiness consists in Wisdom.

Moral Philosophy.—Continuing to feel the strong impulse which it had received from Socrates, philosophy was now for a long while to be almost exclusively moral philosophy. Only it divided very sharply in two directions. Antisthenes and Aristippus were both pupils of Socrates. From Antisthenes came the Cynics; from Aristippus the philosophers of pleasure. The Cynics gave birth to the Stoics, the philosophers of pleasure to the Epicureans, and these two great schools practically divided all antiquity between them. We will take the Epicureans first because, chronologically, they slightly preceded the Stoics.

Epicurus.—Epicurus, born at Athens a little after the death of Plato, brought up at Samos by his parents who had been forced to expatriate themselves owing to reverses of fortune, returned to Athens about 305 B.C., and there founded a school. Personally he was a true wise man, sober, scrupulous, a despiser of pleasure, severe to himself, *in practice* a Stoic. As his general view of the universe he taught approximately the doctrine of Democritus : the world is composed of a multitude of atoms, endowed with certain movements, which attach themselves to one another and combine together, and there is nothing else in the world. Is there not a first cause, a being who set all these atoms in motion, in short, a God ? Epicurus did not think so. Are there gods, as the vulgar believe ? Epicurus believed so ; but he considered that the gods are brilliant, superior, happy creatures, who do not trouble about this world, do not interfere with it, and are even less occupied, were it possible, with mankind. Also they did not create the world, for why should they have created it ? From goodness, said Plato ; but there is so much evil in the world that if they created it from goodness, they were mistaken and must be fools ; and if they willingly permitted evil, they are wicked ; and therefore it is charitable towards them to believe that they did not create it.

Epicurean Morality.—From the ethical point of view Epicurus certainly attaches himself to Aristippus ; but with the difference that lies between pleasure and happiness. Aristippus taught that the aim of life was intelligent pleasure, Epicurus declared that the aim of life was happiness. Now, does happiness consist in pleasures, or does it exclude them ? Epicurus was quite convinced that it excluded them. Like Lord Beaconsfield, he would say, " Life would be almost bearable, were it not for its pleasures." Happiness for Epicurus lay in " phlegm," as Philinte would put it ; it lay in the calm of the mind that has rendered itself inaccessible to every emotion of passion, which is never irritated, never moved, never annoyed, never desires, and never fears. Why, for instance, should we dread death ? So long as we fear it, it is not here ; when it arrives, we shall no longer fear it ; then, why is it an evil ?—But, during life itself, how about sufferings ?—We greatly increase our sufferings by complaints and by self-commiseration. If we acted in the reverse way, if when we were tortured by them we recalled past pleasures and thought of pleasures to come, they would be infinitely mitigated.—But, of what pleasures can a man speak who makes happiness consist in the exclusion of pleasures ?—The pleasures of the wise man are the satisfaction he feels in assuring himself of his own happiness. He finds pleasure when he controls a passion in order to revert to calmness ; he feels pleasure when he converses with his friends about the nature of true happiness ; he feels pleasure when he has diverted a youth from passionate follies or from despair, and brought him back to peace of mind, etc.—But what about sufferings after death?—They do not exist. There is no hell because there is no immortality of the soul. The soul is as material as the body, and dies with it.

You will say, perhaps, that this very severe and austere morality more nearly approaches to Stoicism than to the teaching of Aristippus. This is so true that when Horace confessed with a smile that he returned to the morality of pleasure, he did not say, as we should, "I feel that I am becoming an Epicurean," he said, "I fall back on the precepts of Aristippus"; and Seneca, a professed Stoic, cites Epicurus almost as often as Zeno in his lessons. It may not be quite accurate to state, but there would not be much exaggeration in affirming, that Epicureanism is a smiling Stoicism and Stoicism a gloomy Epicureanism. In the current use of the word we have changed the meaning of Epicurean to make it mean "addicted to pleasure." The warning must be given that there is no more grievous error.

THE VOGUE OF EPICUREANISM.—Epicureanism had an immense vogue in antiquity. The principal professors of it at Athens were Metrodorus, Hermarchus, Polystratus, and Apollodorus. Penetrating to Italy Epicureanism found its most brilliant representative in Lucretius, who of the system made a poem—the admirable *De Natura*

Rerum ; there were also Atticus, Horace, Pliny the younger, and many more. It even became a political opinion : the Cæsarians were Epicureans, the Republicans Stoics. On the appearance of Christianity Epicureanism came into direct opposition with it, and so did Stoicism also ; but in a far less degree. In modern times, as will be seen, Epicureanism has enjoyed a revival.

CHAPTER VIII.

STOICISM.

The Passions are Diseases which can and must be extirpated.

THE LOGIC OF STOICISM.—Stoicism existed as a germ in the Cynic philosophy (and also in Socrates) as did Epicureanism in Aristippus. Zeno was the pupil of Crates. In extreme youth he opened a school at Athens in the Pœcile. The Pœcile was a portico; portico in Greek is *stoa*, hence the name of Stoic. Zeno taught for about thirty years; then, on the approach of age, he died by his own hand. Zeno thought, as did Epicurus and Socrates, that philosophy should only be the science of life and that the science of life lay in wisdom. Wisdom consists in thinking justly and acting rightly; but to think justly only in order to act rightly—which is quite in the spirit of Socrates, and eliminates all the science of research, all consideration of the constitution of the world as well as the total and even the details of matter. Therein is Stoicism more narrow than Epicureanism.

In consequence, man needs clear, precise and severe "logic" (the Stoics were the first to use this word). Armed with this weapon, and only employing it for self-knowledge and self-control, man makes himself wise. The "wise man" of the Stoic is a kind of saint—a superman, as it has since been called—very analogous to his God. All his efforts are concentrated on safeguarding, conquering and suppressing his passions, which are nothing save "diseases of the soul." In the external world he disregards all the "things of chance" — everything, that is, that does not depend on human will—and considers them as non-existent: the ailments of the body, pangs, sufferings, misfortunes and humiliations are not evils, they are things indifferent. On the contrary, crimes and errors are such evils that they are *equally* execrable, and the wise man should reproach himself as severely for the slightest fault as for the greatest crime—a paradoxical doctrine which has aroused the warmth of even respectful opponents of Stoicism, notably Cicero.

MAXIMS OF THE STOICS.—Their most frequently repeated maxim is "abstain and endure"; abstain from all evil, suffer all aggression and so-called misfortune without rebelling or complaining. Another precept widely propagated among them and by them: "live according to nature," remarkably resembles an Epicurean maxim. This must be made clear. This precept as they interpreted it meant: adhere freely and respectfully to the laws of the universe. The world is a God who lives according to the laws He Himself made, and of which we are not judges. These laws surround us and compel us ; sometimes they wound us. We must respect and obey them, have a sort of pious desire that they should operate even against ourselves, and live in reverent conformity with them. Thus understood, the " life in conformity with nature " is nothing else than an aspect of the maxim " endure ! "

Principal Stoics.—The principal adepts and masters of Stoicism with and after Zeno were Cleanthes, Chrysippus, Aristo and Herillus in Greece ; at Rome, Cato, Brutus, Cicero to a certain degree, Thrasea, Epictetus (withal a Greek, who wrote in Greek), Seneca, and finally the Emperor Marcus Aurelius. Stoicism rapidly developed into a religion, having its rites, obediences, ascetic practices, directors of conscience, examination of conscience, and its adepts with a traditional dress, long cloak and long beard. It exerted considerable influence, comparable (comparable only) to Christianity, but it only penetrated the upper and middle classes of society in antiquity without descending, or barely descending, to the masses. Like Epicureanism, Stoicism had a renaissance in modern times in opposition to Christianity : this will be dealt with later.

CHAPTER IX.

ECLECTICS AND SCEPTICS.

Philosophers who wished to belong to no School. Philosophers who decried all Schools and all Doctrines.

THE TWO TENDENCIES.—As might be expected to happen, and as always happens, the multiplicity of sects brought about two tendencies, one consisting in selecting somewhat arbitrarily from each sect what one found best in it, which is called "eclecticism," the other in thinking that no school grasped the truth, that the truth is not to be grasped, which is called "scepticism."

THE ECLECTICS: PLUTARCH.—The Eclectics, who did not form a school, which would have been difficult in the spirit in which they acted, had only this in common, that they venerated the great thinkers of ancient Greece, and that they felt or endeavoured to feel respect and toleration for all religions. They venerated Socrates, Plato, Aristotle, Epicurus, Zeno, Moses, Jesus, St. Paul, and loved to imagine that they were each a partial revelation of the great divine thought, and they endeavoured to reconcile these divergent revelations by proceeding on broad lines and general considerations. Among them were Moderatus, Nicomachus, Nemesius, etc. The most illustrious, without being the most profound—though his literary talent has always kept him prominent—was Plutarch. His chief effort, since then often renewed, was to reconcile reason and faith (I am writing of the polytheistic faith). Perceiving in mythology ingenious allegories, he showed that under the name of allegories covering and containing profound ideas, all polytheism could be accepted by the reason of a Platonist, an Aristotelian, or a Stoic. The Eclectics had not much influence, and only pleased two sorts of minds: those who preferred knowledge rather than conviction, and found in Eclecticism an agreeable variety of points of view; and those who liked to believe a little in everything, and possessing receptive but not steadfast minds were not far from sceptics and who might be called affirmative sceptics in opposition to the negative sceptics: sceptics who say "Heavens, yes," as opposed to sceptics who always say "Presumably, no."

The Sceptics: Pyrrho.—The Sceptics proper were chronologically more ancient. The first famous Sceptic was a contemporary of Aristotle; he followed Alexander on his great expedition into Asia. This was Pyrrho. He taught, as it appears, somewhat obscurely at Athens, and for successor had Timon. These philosophers, like so many others, sought happiness and affirmed that it lay in abstention from decision, in the mind remaining in abeyance, in *aphasia*. Pyrrho being accustomed to say that he was indifferent whether he was alive or dead, on being asked: "Then why do you live?" answered: "Just because it is indifferent whether one lives or is dead." As may be imagined, their favourite sport was to draw the various schools into mutual opposition, to rout some by the rest, to show that all were strong in what they negatived, but weak in what they affirmed, and so to dismiss them in different directions.

THE NEW ACADEMY.—Scepticism, albeit attenuated, softened, and less aggressive, reappeared in a school calling itself the New Academy. It claimed to adhere to Socrates—not without some show of reason, since Socrates had declared that the only thing he knew was that he knew nothing—and the essential tenet of this school was to affirm nothing. Only the Academicians believed that certain things were probable, more probable than others, and they are the founders of probabilism, which is nothing more than conviction accompanied with modesty. They were more or less moderate, according to personal temperament. Arcesilaus was emphatically moderate, and limited himself to the development of the critical faculties of his pupil. Carneades was more negative, and arrived at or reverted to scepticism and sophistry pure and simple. Cicero, with a certain foundation of Stoicism, was a pupil, and one of the most moderate, of the New Academy.

ÆNESIDEMUS : AGRIPPA : EMPIRICUS.—Others built on experience itself, on the incertitude of our sensations and observations, on everything that can cheat us and cause us illusion in order to display how *relative* and how miserably partial is human knowledge. Such was Ænesidemus, whom it might be thought Pascal had read, so much does the latter give the reasons of the former when he is not absorbed in faith, and when he assumes the position of a sceptic precisely in order to prove the necessity of taking refuge in faith. Such was Agrippa ; such, too, was Sextus Empiricus, so often critical of science, who demonstrates (as to a slight extent M. Henri Poincaré does in our own day) that all sciences, even those which like mathematics and geometry are proudest of their certainty, rest upon conventions and intellectual " conveniences."

CHAPTER X.

NEOPLATONISM.

Reversion to Metaphysics. Imaginative Metaphysicians after the manner of Plato, but in excess.

ALEXANDRINISM.—Amid all this, metaphysics—namely, the effort to comprehend the universe—appears somewhat at a discount. It enjoyed a renaissance in the third century of our era among some teachers from Alexandria (hence the name of the Alexandrine school) who came to lecture at Rome with great success. Alexandrinism is a "Neoplatonism"—that is, a renewed Platonism and, as considered by its authors, an augmented one.

PLOTINUS.—Plotinus taught this: God and matter exist. God is one, matter is multiple and divisible. God in Himself is incomprehensible, and is only to be apprehended in his manifestations. Man rises not to comprehension of Him but to the perception of Him by a series of degrees which are, as it were, the progressive purification of faith, and which lead us to a kind of union with Him resembling that of one being with another whom he could never see, but of whose presence he could have no doubt. Matter, that is the universe, is an emanation from God as perfume comes from a flower. All is not God, and only God can be God, but all is divine and all participates in God, just as each of our thoughts participates of our soul. Now, if all emanates from God, all also tends to return to Him, as bodies born of earth, nourished by earth, invigorated by the forces proceeding from the earth, tend to return to the earth. This is what makes the harmony of the world. The law of laws is, that every fragment of the universe derived from God returns to Him and desires to return to Him. The universe is an emanation from the perfect, and an effort towards perfection. The universe is a God in exile who has nostalgia for himself. The universe is a progressive descent from God with a tendency towards reintegration with Him.

How does this emanation from God becoming matter take place ? That is a mystery ; but it may be supposed to take place by successive stages. From God emanates spirit, impersonal spirit which is not spirit of this or that, but universal spirit spread through the whole world and animating it. From spirit emanates the soul, which can unite itself to a body and form an individual. The soul is less divine than spirit, which in turn is less divine than God, but yet retains divinity. From the soul emanates the body to which it unites itself. The body is less divine than the soul, which was less divine than spirit, which was less divine than God; but it still possesses divinity for it has a form, a figure, a design marked and impressed with divine spirit. Finally, matter without form is the most distant of the emanations from God, and the lowest of the descending stages of God. God *is* in Himself; He thinks in pure thought in spirit; He thinks in mixed and confused thought in the soul; He feels in the body; He sleeps in unformed matter. The object of unformed matter is to acquire form, that is a body; and the object of a body is to have a soul; and the aim of a soul is to be united in spirit, and the aim of spirit is to be absorbed into God.

Souls not united to bodies contemplate spirit and enjoy absolute happiness. Other souls not united to bodies, but solicited by a certain instinct to unite themselves to bodies are of ambiguous but still very exalted nature. Souls united to bodies (our own) have descended far, but can raise themselves and be purified by contemplation of the eternal intelligence, and by relative union with it. This contemplation has several degrees, so to speak, of intensity, degrees which Plotinus termed hypostases. By perception we obtain a glimpse of ideas, by dialectics we penetrate them;

by a final hypostasis, which is ecstasy, we can sometimes unite ourselves directly to God and live in Him.

THE PUPILS OF PLOTINUS.—Plotinus had as pupils and successors, amongst others, Porphyry and Iamblichus. Porphyry achieves little except the exposition of the doctrine of his master, and only shows originality as a logician. Iamblichus and his school made a most interesting effort to revive exhausted and expiring paganism and to constitute a philosophic paganism. The philosophers of the school of Iamblichus are, by the way, magicians, charlatans, miracle-mongers, men as antipositivist as possible. Iamblichus himself sought to reconcile polytheism with Neoplatonism by putting in the centre of all a supreme deity, an essential deity from whom he made a crowd of secondary, tertiary, and quaternary deities to emanate, ranging from those purely immaterial to those inherent in matter. The subtle wanderings of Neoplatonism were continued obscurely in the school of Athens until it was closed for ever in 529 by the Emperor Justinian as being hostile to the religion of the Empire, which at that epoch was Christianity.

CHAPTER XI.

CHRISTIANITY.

Philosophic Ideas which Christianity welcomed, adopted or created.
How it must give a fresh Aspect to all Philosophy, even that foreign to itself.

Christian Philosophy and Morality.—Christianity spread through the Empire by the propaganda of the Apostles, and more especially St. Paul, from about the year 40. Its success was extremely rapid, especially among the populace, and little by little it won over the upper classes. As a general philosophy, primitive Christianity did not absolutely bring more than the Hebrew dogmas : the unity of God, a providential Deity, that is, one directly interfering in human affairs ; immortality of the soul with rewards and penalties beyond the grave (a recent theory among the Jews, yet one anterior to Christianity). As a moral system, Christianity brought something so novel and so beautiful that it is not very probable that humanity will ever surpass it, which may be imperfectly and incompletely summed up thus : love of God ; He must not only be feared as He was by the pagans and the ancient Jews ; He must be loved passionately as a son loves his father, and all things must be done for this love and in consideration of this love; all men are brethren as sons of God, and they should love one another as brothers; love your neighbour as yourself, love him who does not love you; love your enemies; be not greedy for the goods of this world, nor ambitious, nor proud; for God loves the lowly, the humble, the suffering, and the miserable, and He will exalt the lowly and put down the mighty from their seats.

Nothing like this had been said in all antiquity, and it needs extraordinary ingenuity (of a highly interesting character, by the way), to find in ancient wisdom even a few traces of this doctrine.

Finally, into politics, so to speak, Christianity brought this novelty: there are two empires, the empire of God and the empire of man; you do not owe everything to the earthly empire; you are bound to give it faithfully only what is needed for it to be strong and preserve society; apart from that, and that done, you are the subject of God and have only to answer to God for your thoughts, your belief, your conscience; and over that portion of yourself the State has neither right nor authority unless it be usurped and tyrannical. And therein lay the charter of individual liberty like the charter of the rights of man.

As appeal to the feelings, Christianity brought

the story of a young God, infinitely good and gentle, who had never cursed, who had been infinitely loved, who had been persecuted and betrayed, who had forgiven his executioners, and who died in great sufferings and who was to be imitated (whence came the thirst for martyrdom). This story in itself is not more affecting than that of Socrates, but it is that of a young martyr and not of an old one, and therein lies a marked difference for the imagination and emotions of the multitude.

The Success of Christianity.—The prodigious rapidity of the success of Christianity is easily explicable. Polytheism had no longer a great hold on the masses, and no philosophic doctrine had found or had even sought the path to the crowd; Christianity, essentially democratic, loved the weak and humble, had a tendency to prefer them to the great ones of this world, and to regard them as being more the children of God, and was therefore received by the masses as the only doctrine which could replace the worm-eaten polytheism. And in Christianity they saw the religion for which they were waiting, and in the heads of Christianity their own protectors and defenders.

Its Evolution.—The evolution of Christianity was very rapid, and from a great moral doctrine with a minimum of rudimentary metaphysics it became, perchance mistakenly, a philosophy giving account, or desirous of giving account, of everything; it so to speak incorporated a metaphysic, borrowed in great part from Greek philosophy, in great part from the Hebrew traditions. It possessed ideas on the origin of matter, and whilst maintaining that God was eternal, denied that matter was, and asserted that God created it out of nothing. It had theories on the essence of God, and saw Him in three Persons, or hypostases, one aspect of God as power, another as love, and the other as intelligence. It presented theories on the incarnation and humanisation of God, God being made man in Jesus Christ without ceasing to be God. It conceived new relationships of man to God, man having in himself powers of purgation and perfection, but always needing divine help for self-perfection (theory of grace). And this he must believe; if not he would feel insolent pride in his freedom. It had ideas about the existence of evil, declaring in "justification of God" for having permitted evil on earth, that the world was a place of trial, and that evil was only a way of putting man to the test and discovering what were his merits. It had its notions on the rewards and penalties beyond the grave, hell for the wicked and heaven for the good, as had been known to antiquity, but added purgatory, a place for both punishment and purification by punishment, an entirely Platonic theory, which Plato may have inspired but did not himself entertain. Finally, it was a complete philosophy answering, and that in a manner often admirable, all the questions that mankind put or could ever put.

And, as so often happens, that has proved a weakness and a strength to it: a weakness because embarrassed with subtle, complicated, insoluble questions wherein mankind will always be involved, it was forced to engage in endless discussions wherein the bad or feeble reasons advanced by this or that votary compromised the whole work; a strength because whoever brings a rule of life is practically compelled to support it by general ideas bearing on the relations of things and to give it a place in a general survey of the world; otherwise he appears impotent, weak, disqualified to give that very rule of life, incapable of replying to the interrogations raised by that rule of life; and finally, lacking in authority.

Schisms and Heresies.—Right or wrong, and it is difficult and highly hazardous to decide the question, Christianity was a complete philosophy, which was why it had its schisms and heresies, a certain number of sincere Christians not resolving the metaphysical questions in the way of the majority. Heresies were innumerable; only the two shall be cited which are deeply interesting in the history of philosophy. Manes, an Arab (and Arabia was then a Persian province), revived the old Zoroastrian doctrine of two principles of good and evil, and saw in the world two contending gods, the God of perfection and the god of sin, and laid upon man the duty of assisting the God of goodness so that His kingdom should come and cause the destruction of evil in the world. From him proceeded the Manicheans, who exerted great influence and were condemned by many Councils until their sect died out, only to reappear or seem to reappear fairly often in the middle ages and in modern times.

Arius denied the Trinity, believing only in one God, not only unique, but in one Person, and in consequence denied the divinity of Jesus Christ. He was perpetually involved in controversies and polemics, supported by some Bishops, opposed by the majority. After his death his doctrine spread strangely. It was stifled in the East by Theodosius, but was widely adopted by the "barbarians" of the West (Goths, Vandals, Burgundians, Lombards). It was revived, more or less exactly, after the Reformation, among the Socinians.

ROME AND CHRISTIANITY.—The relations of

Christianity with the Roman government were in the highest degree tragic, as is common knowledge. There were ten sanguinary persecutions, some being atrocious. It has often been asked what the cause was of this animosity against the Christians on the part of a government which tolerated all religions and all philosophies. Persecutions were natural at Athens where a democracy, obstinately attached to the local deities, treated as enemies of the country those who did not take these gods into consideration ; persecutions were natural on the part of a Calvin or a Louis XIV who combined in themselves the two authorities and would not admit that anyone in the State had the right to think differently from its head ; but it has been argued that they were incomprehensible on the part of a government which admitted all cults and all doctrines. The explanation perhaps primarily lies in the fact that Christianity was essentially popular, and that the government saw in it not only plebeianism, which was disquieting, but an organisation of plebeianism, which was still more so. The administration of religion had always been in the hands of the aristocracy ; the Roman pontiffs were patricians, the Emperor was the sovereign pontiff ; to yield obedience, even were it only spiritually, to private men as priests was to be disobedient to the Roman aristocracy, to the Emperor himself, and was properly speaking a revolt.

A further explanation, perhaps, is that each new religion that was introduced at Rome did not oppose and did not contradict polytheism, the principle of polytheism being precisely that there are many gods; whereas Christianity denying all those gods and affirming that there is only one, and that all others must be despised as non-existent, inveighed against, denied and ruined or threatened to destroy the very essence of polytheism. It was not a variation, it was a heresy; it was more than heretical, it was anarchical; it did not only condemn this or that religion, but even the very tolerance with which the Roman government accepted all religions. Hence it is natural enough that it should have been combatted to the utmost by practically all the Emperors, from the most execrable, such as Nero, to the best, such as Marcus Aurelius.

Christianity and the Philosophers.—The relations of Christianity with philosophy were confused. The immense majority of philosophers rejected it, considering their own views superior to it, and moreover, feeling it to be formidable, made use against it of all that could be found beautiful, specious, or expedient in ancient philosophy; and the ardour of Neoplatonism, which we have considered, in part arose from precisely this instinct of rivalry and of struggle. At that epoch there was a throng of men like Ernest Havet presenting Hellenism in opposition to Christianity, and Ernest Havet is only a Neoplatonist of the nineteenth century.

A certain number of philosophers, nevertheless, either on the Jewish-Christian side or on the Hellenic, tried some reconciliation either as Jews making advances to Hellenism or as Greeks admitting there was something acceptable on the part of Sion. Aristobulus, a Jew (prior to Jesus Christ), seems to have endeavoured to bring Moses into agreement with Plato; Philo (a Jew contemporary with and surviving Jesus Christ and a non-Christian), about whom there is more information, throughout his life pursued the plan of demonstrating all the resemblances he could discover between Plato and the Old Testament, much in the same way as in our time some have striven to point out the surprising agreement of the Darwinian theory with Genesis. He was called the Jewish Plato, and at Alexandria it was said: "Philo imitates Plato or Plato imitates Philo."

On their side, later on, certain eclectic Greeks already cited, Moderatus, Nicomachus, Nemesius, extended goodwill so far as to take into account, if not Jesus, at least Moses, and to admit Israelitish thought into the history of philosophy and of human wisdom. But, in general it was by the schools of philosophy and by the ever dwindling section of society priding itself upon its philosophy that Christianity was most decisively repulsed, thrust on one side and misunderstood.

CHRISTIAN PHILOSOPHERS.—Without dealing with many others who belong more especially to the history of the Church rather than to that of philosophy, the Christians did not lack two very illustrious philosophers who must receive attention—Origen and St. Augustine.

ORIGEN.—Origen was a native of Alexandria at the close of the second century, and a pupil of St. Clement of Alexandria. A Christian and a Platonist, in order to give himself permission and excuse for reconciling the two doctrines, he alleged that the Apostles had only given so much of the Christian teaching as the multitude could comprehend, and that the learned could interpret it in a manner more subtle, more profound, and more complete. Having observed this precaution, he revealed his system, which was this: God is a pure spirit. He already has descended one step in *spirits*, which are emanations from Him. These spirits are capable of good and evil. When addicted to evil, they clothe themselves with matter and become souls in bodies. Which is what we are. There are others lower than ourselves. There are impure spirits which have clothed themselves with unclean bodies; these are demons. Now, as the fallen brethren of angels, we are free, less free than they, but still free. Through this freedom we can in our present existence either raise or lower ourselves. But this freedom does not suffice us; a little help is essential. This help comes to us from the spirits which have remained pure. The help they afford us is opposed by the efforts of the utterly fallen spirits who are lower in the scale than ourselves. To combat these fallen spirits, to help the pure spirits who help us, and to help them to help us, such is our duty in this life, which is a medicine, the medicine of Plato, namely a punishment; sterile when it is not accepted by us, salutary when gratefully accepted by us, it then becomes expiation and in consequence purification. The part of the Redeemer in all this is the same as that of the spirits, but on a grander and more decisive plane. King of spirits, Spirit of spirits, by revelation He illumines our confused intelligence and fortifies our weak will against temptation.

St. Augustine.—St. Augustine of Tagaste (in

Africa), long a pagan exercising the profession of professor of rhetoric, became a Christian and was Bishop of Hippo. It is he who " fixed " the Christian doctrine in the way most suitable to and most acceptable to western intelligence. Instead of confusing it, more or less intentionally, more or less inadvertently, with philosophy, he exerted all his great talents to make the most precise distinction from it. Philosophers (he says) have always regarded the world as an emanation from God. Then all is God. Such is not the way to reason. There is no emanation, but creation; God created the world and has remained distinct from it. He lives in it in such a way that we live in Him; in Him, we live and move and have our being; He dwells throughout the world, but He is not the world; He is everywhere but He is not all. God created the world. Then, can it be said that before the world was created God remained doing nothing during an immense space of time? Certainly not, because time only began at the creation of the world. God is outside time. The eternal is the absence of time. God, therefore, was not an instant before He created the world. Or, if it be preferred, there was an eternity before the birth of the world. But it is the same thing; for eternity is the non-existence of time.

Some understand God in three Persons as three Gods. This polytheism, this paganism must be rejected. But how to understand ? How ? You feel in yourself several souls ? No. And yet there are several faculties of the soul. The three Persons of God are the three divine faculties. Man has body and soul. No one ought to have doubts about the soul, for to have doubts presupposes thought, and to think is to be ; above all things we are thinking beings. But what is the soul ? Something immaterial, assuredly, since it can conceive immaterial things, such as a line, a point, surface, space. It is as necessary for the soul to be immaterial in order to be able to grasp the immaterial, as it is necessary for the hand to be material in order that it can grasp a stone.

Whence comes the soul ? From the souls of ancestors by transmission ? This is not probable, for this would be to regard it as material. From God by emanation ? This is inadmissible ; it is the same error as believing that the world emanates from God. Here, too, there is no emanation, but creation. God creates the souls in destination for bodies themselves born from heredity. Once the body is destroyed, what becomes of the soul ? It cannot perish ; for thought not being dependent upon the senses, there is no reason for its disappearance on the disappearance of the senses.

Human liberty is an assured fact ; we are free to do good or evil. But then God has not been able to know in advance what I shall do to-day, and in consequence God, at least in His knowledge, has limitations, is not omnipotent. St. Augustine replies confusedly (for the question is undoubtedly insoluble) that we have an illusion of liberty, an illusion that we are free, which suffices for us to acquire merit if we do right and demerit if we do wrong, and that this illusion of liberty is a relative liberty, which leaves the prescience of God, and therefore His omnipotence, absolute. Man is also extremely weak, debilitated, and incapable of good on account of original sin, the sin of our first parents, which is transmitted to us through heredity and paralyses us. But God helps us, and this is what is termed grace. He helps us gratuitously, as is indicated by the word " grace " —if He wishes and when He wishes and in the measure that He wishes. From this arises the doctrine of " predestination," by which it is preordained whether a man is to be saved or lost.

PART II.

IN THE MIDDLE AGES.

F

CHAPTER I.

FROM THE FIFTH CENTURY TO THE THIRTEENTH.

**Philosophy is only an Interpreter of Dogma.
When it is declared contrary to Dogma by the Authority of Religion, it is a Heresy.
Orthodox and Heterodox Interpretations.
Some independent Philosophers.**

DOGMA.—After the invasion of the barbarians, philosophy, like literature, sought refuge in monasteries and in the schools which prelates instituted and maintained near them. But the Church does not permit the free search for truth. The truth has been established by the Fathers of the Church and fixed by the Councils. Thenceforth the philosophic life, so to speak, which had never been interrupted, assumed a fresh character. Within the Church it sheltered—I will not say disguised—itself under the interpretation of dogma; it became a sort of respectful auxiliary of theology, and was accordingly called the "handmaid of theology," *ancilla theologiae.* When emancipated, when departing from dogma, it is a "heresy," and all the great heresies are nothing else than schools of philosophy, which is why heresies must come into a history of philosophy. And at last, but only towards the close of the middle ages, lay thought without disturbing itself about dogma and no longer thinking about its interpretation, created philosophic doctrines exactly as the philosophers of antiquity invented them apart from religion, to which they were either hostile or indifferent.

SCHOLASTICISM: SCOTUS ERIGENA.—The orthodox philosophy of the middle ages was the scholastic. Scholasticism consisted in amassing and in making known scientific facts and matters of knowledge which it was useful for a well-bred man not to be ignorant of, and with this purpose encyclopædias were constructed; on the other hand, it consisted not precisely in the reconciliation of faith with reason, not precisely and far less in the submission of faith to the criticism of reason, but in making faith sensible to reason, as had been the office of the Fathers of the Church, more especially St. Augustine.

Scotus Erigena, a Scotsman attached to the Palatine Academy of Charles the Bald, lived in the eleventh century. He was extremely learned. His philosophy was Platonic, or rather the bent of his mind was Platonic. God is the absolute Being; He is unnameable, since any name is a delimitation of the being; He *is* absolutely and infinitely. As the creator of all and uncreated, He is the cause *per se*; as the goal to which all things tend, He is the supreme end. The human soul is of impenetrable essence like God Himself; accordingly, it is God in us. We have fallen through the body and, whilst in the flesh, we can, by virtue and more especially by the virtue of penitence, raise ourselves to the height of the angels. The world is the continuous creation of God. It must not be said that God created the world, but that He creates it; for if He ceased from sustaining it, the world would no longer exist. God is perpetual creation and perpetual attraction. He draws all beings to Himself, and in the end He will have them all in Himself. There is predestination to perfection in everything.

These theories, some of which, as has been seen, go beyond dogma and form at least the beginning of heresy, are all impregnated with Platonism, especially with Neoplatonism, and lead to the supposition that Scotus Erigena possessed very wide Greek learning.

ARABIAN SCIENCE.—A great literary and philosophical fact in the eighth century was the invasion of the Arabs. Mahometans successively invaded Syria, Persia, Africa, and Spain, forming a crescent the two points of which touched the two extremities of Europe. Inquisitive and sagacious pupils of the Greeks in Africa and Asia, they founded everywhere brilliant Universities which rapidly acquired renown (Bagdad, Bassorah, Cordova, Grenada, Seville, Murcia) and brought to Europe a new quota of science; for instance, all the works of Aristotle, of which western Europe possessed practically nothing. Students greedy for knowledge came to learn from them in Spain; for instance, Gerbert, who developed into a man of great learning, who taught at Rheims and became Pope. Individually the Arabs were often great philosophers, and at least the names must be mentioned of Avicenna (a Neoplatonist of the tenth century) and Averroes (an Aristotelian of the twelfth century who betrayed tendencies towards admitting the eternity of nature, and its evolution through its own initiative during the course of time). Their doctrines were propagated, and the ancient books which they made known became widely diffused. From them dates the sway of Aristotle throughout the middle ages.

St. Anselm.—St. Anselm, in the eleventh century, a Savoyard, who was long Abbot of Bec in Normandy and died Archbishop of Canterbury, is one of the most illustrious doctors of philosophy in the service of theology that ever lived. "A new St. Augustine" (as he has been called), he starts from faith to arrive at faith after it has been rendered sensible to reason. Like St. Augustine he says: "I believe in order to understand" (well persuaded that if I never believed I should never understand), and he adds what had been in the thought of St. Augustine: "I understand in order to believe." St. Anselm proved the existence of God by the most abstract arguments. For example, "It is necessary to have a cause, one or multiple; one is God; multiple, it can be derived from one single cause, and that one cause is God; it can be a particular cause in each thing caused; but then it is necessary to suppose a personal force which must itself have a cause and thus we work back to a common cause, that is to say to a single one."

He proved God again by the proof which has remained famous under the name of the argument of St. Anselm: To conceive God is to prove that He is; the conception of God is proof of His existence; for every idea has its object; above all, an idea which has infinity for object takes for granted the existence of infinity; for all being finite here below, what would give the idea of infinity to the human mind? Therefore, if the human brain has the idea of infinity it is because of the existence of infinity. The argument is perhaps open to difference of opinion, but as proof of a singular vigour of mind on the part of its author, it is indisputable.

Highly intellectual also is his explanation of the necessity of redemption. *Cur Deus Homo?* (the title of one of his works) asked St. Anselm. Because sin in relation to an infinite God is an infinite crime. Man, finite and limited in capacity, could therefore never expiate it. Then what could God do to avenge His honour and to have satisfaction rendered to Him? He could only make Himself man without ceasing to be God, in order that as man He should offer to God a reparation to which as God He would give the character of infinitude. It was therefore absolutely necessary that at a given moment man should become God, which could only be done upon the condition that God made himself man.

REALISTS: NOMINALISTS: CONCEPTUALISTS.—It was in the time of St. Anselm that there arose the celebrated philosophic quarrel between the "realists, nominalists, and conceptualists." It is here essential to employ these technical terms or else not to allude to the dispute at all, because the strife is above all a war of words. The realists (of whom St. Anselm was one), said: "The ideas (idea of virtue, idea of sin, idea of greatness, idea of littleness) are realities; they exist, in a spiritual manner of course, but they really exist; they are: there is a virtue, a sin, a greatness, a littleness, a reason, etc. (and this was an exact reminiscence of the ideas of Plato). It is indeed only the idea, the general, the universal, which is real, and the particular has only the appearance of reality. Men do not exist, the individual man does not exist; what exists is 'man' in general, and individual men are only the appearance of—the coloured reflections of—the universal man." The nominalists (Roscelin the Canon of Compiègne, for instance) answered: "No; the general ideas, the universals as you say, are only names, are only words, emissions of the voice, labels, if you like, which we place on such and such categories of facts observed by us; there is no greatness; there are a certain number of great things, and when we think of them we inscribe this word 'greatness' on the general idea which we conceive. 'Man' does not exist; there are men and the word humanity is only a word which to us represents a collective idea."

Why did the realists cling so to their universals, held to be realities and the sole realities? For many reasons. If the individual alone be real, there are not three Persons in the Godhead, there are three Gods and the unity of God is not real, it is only a word, and God is not real, He is only an utterance of the voice. If the individual is not real, the Church is not real; she does not exist, there only exist Christians who possess freedom of thought and of faith. Now the Church is real and it is not only desirable that she should be real, but even that she alone should possess reality and that the individuals constituting her should exist by her and not by themselves. (This is precisely the doctrine with regard to society now current among certain philosophers: society exists independently of its members; it has laws of its own independently of its members; it is a reality on its own basis; and its members are by it, not it by them, and therefore they should obey it; M. Durckheim is a "realist").

Abelard of Nantes, pupil of the nominalist, William of Champeaux, learned man, artist, man of letters, an incomparable orator, tried to effect a conciliation. He said: "the universal is not a reality, certainly; but it is something more than a simple word; it is a conception of the mind, which is something more than an utterance of the voice. As conception of the mind, in fact, it lives with a life which goes beyond the individual, because it can be common to several individuals, to many individuals, and because in fact it is common to them. The general idea that I have and which I have communicated to my hearers, and which returns to me from my hearers, is more than a word since it is a link between my hearers and myself, and an atmosphere in which I and my hearers live. Is the Church only to be a word? God forbid that I should say so. She is a bond between all Christians; she is a general idea common to them all, so that in her each individual feels himself several, feels himself many; although it is true that were she not believed in by anyone she would be nothing." At bottom he was a nominalist, but more shrewd, more subtle, also more profound and more precise, having a better grasp of what William of Champeaux had desired to say. He shared in his condemnation.

Apart from the great dispute, his ideas were singularly broad and bold. Half knowing, half guessing at ancient philosophy, he held it in high esteem; he found there, because he delighted in finding there, all the Christian ideas; the one God, the Trinity, the Incarnation, the imputation of the merits of the saints, original sin; and he found less of a gulf between ancient philosophy and Christianity than between the Old and the New Testaments (this is because the only Christianity known to Abelard, not the primitive but that constituted in the fourth century, was profoundly impregnated with Hellenism). He believed the Holy Ghost to have revealed himself to the wise men of antiquity as well as to the Jews and the Christians, and that virtuous pagans may have been saved. The moral philosophy of Abelard is very elevated and pure. Our acts proceed from God; for it is impossible that they should not; but He permits us the faculty of disobedience "in order that virtue may exist," to which it tends; for if the tendency to evil did not exist, there would be no possibility of effort against evil, and if no efforts, then no virtue; God, who cannot be virtuous since He cannot be tempted by evil, can be virtuous in man, which is why He leaves him the tendency to evil for him to triumph over it and be virtuous so that virtue may exist; even if He were Himself to lead us into temptation, the tendency would still be the same; He would only lead us into it to give us the opportunity for struggle and victory, and therefore in order that virtue might exist; the possibility of sin is the condition of virtue, and in consequence, even in the admission of this possibility and above all by its admission, God is virtuous.

The bad deed, furthermore, is not the most considerable from the point of view of guilt; as merit or demerit the intention is worth as much as the deed and he is criminal who has had the intention to be so (which is clearly according to the Gospel).

HUGO DE SAINT-VICTOR: RICHARD.—Abelard possessed perhaps the broadest and greatest mind of the whole of the middle ages. After these famous names must be mentioned Hugo de Saint-Victor, a somewhat obscure mystic of German origin; and the not less mystical Richard, who, thoroughly persuaded that God is not attained by reason but by feeling, taught exaltation to Him by detachment from self and by six degrees: renunciation, elevation, impulsion, precipitation, ecstasy, and absorption.

CHAPTER II.

THE THIRTEENTH CENTURY.

Influence of Aristotle.
His Adoption by the Church. Religious Philosophy of St. Thomas Aquinas.

ARISTOTLE AND THE CHURCH.—From the thirteenth century, Aristotle, completely known and translated into Latin, was adopted by the Church and became in some sort its lay vicar. He was regarded, and I think rightly, as of all the Greek thinkers the least dangerous to her and as the one to whom could be left all the scientific instruction whilst she reserved to herself all the religious teaching. Aristotle, in fact, " defended her from Plato," in whom were always found some germs of adoration of this world, or some tendencies in this direction, in whom was also found a certain polytheism much disguised, or rather much purified, but actual and dangerous; therefore, from the moment when it became necessary to select, Aristotle was tolerated and finally invested with office.

ST. THOMAS AQUINAS.—As Aristotelian theologians must be cited William of Auvergne, Vincent of Beauvais, Albertus Magnus; but the sovereign name of this period of the history of philosophy is St. Thomas Aquinas. St. Thomas Aquinas wrote several small works but, surpassing them all, the *Summa* (encyclopædia) which bears his name. In general philosophy St. Thomas Aquinas is an Aristotelian, bending but not distorting the ideas of Aristotle to Christian conceptions. Like Aristotle, he demonstrated God by the existence of motion and the necessity of a first motive power; he further demonstrated it by the contingent, relative, and imperfect character of all here below: "there is in things more or less goodness, more or less truth." But we only affirm the more or less of a thing by comparing it with something absolute and as it approaches more or less to this absolute; there is therefore an absolute being, namely God—and this argument appeared to him better than that of St. Anselm, which he refuted.

His conception of Nature.—He showed the whole of nature as a great hierarchy, proceeding from the least perfect and the most shapeless to the most complete and determinate; from another aspect, as separated into two great kingdoms, that of necessity (mineral, vegetable, animal), and that of grace (humanity). He displayed it willed by God, projected by God, created by God; governed by God according to antecedent and consequent wills, that is, by general wills

(God desires man to be saved) and by particular wills (God wishes the sinner to be punished), and the union of the general wills is the creation, and the result of all the particular wills is Providence. Nature and man with it are the work not only of the power but of the goodness of God, and it is by love that He created us and we must render Him love for love, which is involuntarily done by Nature herself in her obedience to His laws, and which we must do voluntarily by obedience to His commandments.

The Soul.—Our soul is immaterial and more complete than that of animals, for St. Thomas does not formally deny that animals have souls ; the instinct of animals is the sensitive soul according to Aristotle, which is capable of four faculties : sensibility, imagination, memory, and estimation, that is elementary intelligence : " the bird picks up straw, not because it gratifies her feelings [not by a movement of sensibility], but because it serves to make her nest. It is therefore necessary that an animal should perceive those intuitions which do not come within the scope of the senses. It is by opinion or estimation that it perceives these intuitions, these distant ends." We, mankind, possess a soul which is sensibility, imagination, memory, and reason. Reason is the faculty not only of having ideas, but of establishing connections and chains of connection between the ideas and of conceiving general ideas. Reason pauses before reaching God because the idea of God precisely is the only one which cannot be brought to the mind by the inter-relation of ideas, for God surpasses all ideas; the idea of God is given by faith, which can be subsequently helped by reason, for the latter can work to make faith perceptible to reason.

Our soul is full of passions, divisible into two great categories, the passions of desire and those of anger. The passions of desire are rapid or violent movements towards some object which seems to us a good; the passions of anger are movements of revolt against something which opposes our movement towards a good. The common root of all the passions is love, for it is obvious that from it are derived the passions of desire; and as for the passions of wrath they would not exist if we had no love of anything, in which case our desire not coming into collision would not turn into revolt against the obstacle. We are free to do good or evil, to master our evil passions and to follow those of which reason approves. Here reappears the objection of the knowledge God must have beforehand of our actions: if God foresees our actions we are not free; if free, we act contrary to his previsions, then He is not all-powerful.

St. Thomas makes answer thus: "There is not prevision, there is vision, because we are in time whereas God is in eternity. He sees at one glance and instantaneously all the past, present, and future. Therefore, He does not foresee but *see*, and this vision does not hinder human freedom any more than being seen acting prevents one from acting. Because God knows our deeds after they are done, no one can plead that that prevents our full liberty to do them; if He knew them before it is the same as knowing them after, because for Him past, present, and future are all the same moment." This appears subtle but is not, for it only amounts to the statement that in speaking of God time must not be mentioned, for God is as much outside time as outside space.

THE MORAL SYSTEM OF ST. THOMAS.—The very detailed and circumstantial moral system of St. Thomas may thus be summarized: there is in conscience, first, an intellectual act which is the distinction between good and evil; secondly, an act of will which leads us to the good. This power for good urges the practice of virtue. There are human virtues, well known to the ancient philosophers, temperance, courage, wisdom, justice, which lead to happiness on earth; there are divine virtues, inspired in man by God, which are faith, hope, and charity, and they lead to eternal happiness. We practise the virtues, when we are well-disposed, because we are free; but our liberty and our will do not suffice; it is necessary for God to help us, and that is "grace."

FAITH AND REASON.—On the question of the relation of reason to faith, St. Thomas Aquinas recognises, or rather proclaims, that reason will never demonstrate faith, that the revealed truths, the Trinity, original sin, grace, etc., are above reason and infinitely exceed it. How, then, can one believe? By will, aided by the grace of God. Then henceforth must no appeal be made to reason? Yes, indeed! Reason serves to refute the errors of the adversaries of the faith, and by this refutation to confirm itself in belief. The famous *Credo ut intelligam*—I believe in order to understand—is therefore true. Comprehension is only possible on condition of belief; but subsequently comprehension helps to believe, if not more, at least with a greater precision and in a more abundant light. St. Thomas Aquinas here is in exactly the position which Pascal seems to have taken up: Believe and you will understand; understand and you will believe more exactly. Therefore an act of will: "I wish to believe" —a grace of God fortifying this will: faith exists —studies and reasoning: faith is the clearer.

St. Bonaventura: Raymond Lulle.—Beside these men of the highest brain-power there are found in the thirteenth century mystics, that is, poets and eccentrics, both by the way most interesting. It was St. Bonaventura who, being persuaded, almost like an Alexandrine, that one rises to God by synthetic feeling and not by series of arguments, and that one journeys towards Him by successive states of the soul each more pure and more passionate—wrote *The Journey of the Soul to God,* which is, so to speak, a manual of mysticism. Learned as he was, whilst pursuing his own purpose, he digressed in agreeable and instructive fashion into the realms of real knowledge.

Widely different from him, Raymond Lulle or de Lulle, an unbridled schoolman, in his *Ars magna* invented a reasoning machine, analogous to an arithmetical machine, in which ideas were automatically deduced from one another as the figures inscribe themselves on a counter. As often happens, the excess of the method was its own criticism, and an enemy of scholasticism could not have more ingeniously demonstrated that it was a kind of mechanism. Raymond de Lulle was at once a learned man and a well-informed and most enquiring naturalist for whom Arabian science held no secrets. With that he was poet, troubadour, orator, as well as very eccentric and attractive. He was beloved and persecuted in his lifetime and long after his death still found enthusiastic disciples.

BACON.—Contemporaneously lived the man whom it is generally the custom to regard as the distant precursor of experimental science, Roger Bacon (who must not be confused with Francis Bacon, another learned man who lived much nearer to our own time). Roger Bacon, a Franciscan friar, occupied himself almost exclusively with physical and natural science. He passed the greater portion of his life in prison by reason of alleged sorcery and, more especially, perhaps, because he had denounced the evil lives of his brethren. He had at least a presentiment of almost all modern inventions: gunpowder, magnifying glass, telescope, air-pump; he was distinctly an inventor in optics. In philosophy, properly speaking, he denounced what was hollow and empty in scholasticism, detesting that preference should be given to "the straw of words rather than to the grain of fact," and proclaiming that reasoning "is good to conclude but not to establish." Without discovering the law of progress, as has too often been alleged, he arrived at the conclusion that antiquity being the youth of the world, the moderns are the adults, which only meant that it would be at our school that the ancients would learn were they to return to earth and that we ought not to believe blindly in the ancients ; and this was an insurrection against the principle of authority and against the idolatry of Aristotle. He preached the direct study of nature, observation, and experiment with the subsequent application of deduction, and especially of mathematical deduction, to experiment and observation. With all that, he believed in astrology ; for those who are in advance of their time none the less belong to it : but he was a very great man.

CHAPTER III.

THE FOURTEENTH AND FIFTEENTH CENTURIES.

Decadence of Scholasticism. Forebodings of the coming Era. Great Moralists. The Kabbala. Sorcery.

DECADENCE OF SCHOLASTICISM.—The fourteenth century dated the decadence of scholasticism, but saw little new. "Realism" was generally abandoned, and the field was swept by "nominalism," which was the theory that ideas only have existence in the brains which conceive them. Thus Durand de Saint-Pourçain remains famous for having said "to exist is to be individually," which at that epoch was very audacious. William of Ockham repeated the phrase with emphasis; there is nothing real except the individual. That went so far as to cast suspicion on all metaphysics, and somewhat on theology. In fact, *although a devout believer*, Ockham rejected theology, implored the Church not to be learned, because her science proved nothing, and to content herself with faith: "Science belongs to God, faith to men." But, or rather in addition, if the ministers of God were no longer imposing because of their ambitious science, it was necessary for them to regain their sway over souls by other and better means. It was incumbent on them to be saintly, to revert to the purity, the simplicity, and the divine childishness of the primitive Church; and here he was virtually a forerunner of the Reformation.

Ockham was indeed one of the auxiliaries of Philip the Fair in his struggle with the Holy See, suffered excommunication and sought refuge with the Duke of Bavaria, the foe of the Pope.

BURIDAN: THE LIBERTY OF INDIFFERENCE.—Realists and nominalists continued their mutual strife, sometimes physically even, until the middle of the fifteenth century. But nominalism always gained ground, having among other celebrated champions, Peter d'Ailly and Buridan; the one succeeded in becoming Chancellor of the University of Paris, the other in becoming its Rector. Buridan has remained famous through his death and his donkey, both alike legendary. According to a ballad by Villon, Buridan having been too tenderly loved by Joan of Navarre, wife of Philip the Fair, was by his order "thrown in a sack into the Seine." By comparison of dates, the fact seems impossible. According to tradition, either in order to show the freedom of indifference, or that animals are mere machines, Buridan declared that an ass with two baskets full of corn placed one on each side of him and at equal distance from him, would never decide from which he should feed and would die of starvation. Nothing of the kind is to be found in his works, but he may have said so in a lecture and his pupils remembering it have handed it down as a proverb.

PETER D'AILLY: GERSON.—Peter d'Ailly, a highly important ecclesiastic, head of the College of Navarre, chevalier of the University of Paris, Cardinal, a leader in the discussions at the Councils at Pisa and Constance, a drastic reformer of the morals and customs of the Church, did not evince any marked originality as a philosopher, but maintained the already known doctrines of nominalism with extraordinary dialectical skill.

Among his pupils he numbered Gerson, who was also Chancellor of the University of Paris, another highly zealous and energetic reformer, a more avowed enemy of scholasticism and mysticism, of exaggerated austerity and astrology, eminently modern in the best sense of the word, whose political and religious enemies are his title of respect. He was the author of many small books devoted to the popularization of science, religion, and morality. To him was long attributed the *Imitation of Jesus Christ*, which on the whole bears no resemblance to his writings, but which he might very well have written in old age in his retreat in the peaceful silence of the Celestines of Lyons.

THE KABBALA.—From the beginning of the fifteenth century the Renaissance was heralded by a revival of Platonism, both in philosophy and literature. But it was a Platonism strangely understood, a quaint medley of Pythagoreanism and Alexandrinism, the source of which is not very clear (the period not having been much studied). Then arose an incredible infatuation for the Kabbala—a doctrine which was for a long while the secret of the Jews, brooded over by them so to speak during the darkness of the Middle Ages, in which are to be found traces of the most sublime speculations and of the basest superstitions of antiquity. It contained a kind of pantheistic theology closely analogous to those of Porphyry and Iamblichus, as well as processes of magic mingled with astrology. The Kabbalists believe that the sage, who by his astrological knowledge is brought into relation with the celestial powers, can affect nature, alter the course of phenomena, and work miracles. The Kabbala forms part of the history of the marvellous and of occult science rather than of the history of philosophy. Nevertheless men of real learning were initiated and were infatuated, among them the marvellous Pico della Mirandola, Reuchlin, not less remarkable as humanist and Hebraist, who would have run grave risk at the hands of the

Inquisition at Cologne if he had not been saved by Leo X. Cardan, a mathematician and physician, was one of the learned men of that day most impregnated with Kabbalism. He believed in a kind of infallibility of the inner sense, of the intuition, and regarded as futile all sciences that proceeded by slow rational operations. He believed himself a mage and magician. From vanity he spoke of himself in the highest terms and from cynicism in the lowest. Doubt has been cast on his sincerity and also on his sanity.

MAGIC. — There were also Paracelsus and Agrippa. Paracelsus, like Cardan, believed in an intense light infinitely superior to bestial reasoning and calls to mind certain philosophy of intuition of the present day. He too believed himself a magician and physician, and effected cures by the application of astrology to therapeutics. Agrippa did the same with yet stranger phantasies, passing from absolute scepticism through mysticism to magic and demonology; in his own time and in subsequent centuries enjoying the reputation of a devil incarnate as man.

CHAPTER IV.

THE SIXTEENTH CENTURY.

**It is fairly accurate to consider that from the point of view of Philosophy, the Middle Ages lasted until Descartes.
Free-thinkers more or less disguised.
Partisans of Reason apart from Faith, of Observation, and of Experiment.**

THE FREEDOM OF PHILOSOPHY : POMPONAZZO.— The freedom and even the audacity of philosophy rapidly increased. Learned and convinced Aristotelians were bent, either from sheer love of truth or from a more secret purpose, on demonstrating to what extent Aristotle, accurately read, was opposed to the teaching of the Church. For instance, Pomponazzo revealed that nothing could be drawn from Aristotle in favour of the immortality of the soul, in which he himself believed fervently, but in which Aristotle did not believe, hence it was necessary to choose between the Church and Aristotle ; that without the immortality of the soul there could be no rewards beyond the grave, which was entirely his own opinion, but whoever should desire to offer excuses for Aristotle could say it was precisely the existence of punishments and rewards which deprived virtue of existence, which did away with virtue, since the good that is done for the sake of reward or from fear of punishment is no longer good; that, still according to Aristotle, there could never be miracles; that he, Pomponazzo, believed in all the miracles recorded in the Scriptures; but that Aristotle would not have believed in them, and could not have believed in them, a fact which demanded consideration, not assuredly in order to reject belief in miracles, but in order not to bestow on Aristotle that confidence which for so long had been too readily placed in him.

In the same way, he took up again the eternal question of the prescience of God and of human liberty, and showed that no matter what had been said it was necessary to choose: either we are free and God is not omnipotent, or God is omnipotent and we are not free. To regard as true this latter hypothesis, towards which the philosopher evidently leans, would cause God to be the author of evil and of sin. It would not be impossible for God to be the author of evil as an essential condition of good, for if evil were not to exist then there could not be good; nor would it be impossible that He should be the author, not of sin, but of the possibility of sin in order that virtue might be possible, there being no virtue where it is impossible to commit sin; but therein lies a mystery which faith alone can solve, and which Aristotle at any rate has not solved, therefore let us not place reliance on Aristotle.

This disguised free-thinker, for he does not appear to me to be anything else, was one of the most original thinkers of the period intermediate between the Middle Ages and Descartes.

MICHAEL SERVETUS: VANINI.—Such instances of temerity were sometimes fatal to their authors. Michael Servetus, a very learned Spanish physician who perhaps discovered the circulation of the blood before Harvey, disbelieved in the Trinity and in the divinity of Jesus, and, as he was a Platonist, perceived no intermediaries between God and man save ideas. Persecuted by the Catholics, he sought refuge at Geneva, believing Calvin to be more merciful than the Inquisitors, and Calvin burnt him alive.

Vanini, half a century later, that is at the commencement of the seventeenth, a restless, vain and insolent man, after a life full of sudden changes of fortune, and yet distinguished, was burnt alive at Toulouse for certain passages in his *De admirandis . . . arcanis*, and for having said that he would not express his opinion on the immortality of the soul until he was old, a Jew and a German.

Bruno : Campanella.— Giordano Bruno, an astronomer and one of the first to affirm that the sun was the centre of the world, professed, despite certain precautions, a doctrine which confused God with the world and denied or excluded creation. Giordano Bruno was arrested at Venice in 1593, kept seven years in prison and finally burnt at Rome in 1600.

Campanella, likewise an Italian, who spent twenty-seven years in a dungeon for having conspired against the Spanish masters of his country, and who died in exile in Paris in 1639, was a sceptic in philosophy, or rather an antimetaphysician, and, as would be said nowadays, a positivist. There are only two sources of knowledge, observation and reasoning. Observation makes us know things—is this true ? May not the sensations of things which we have be a simple phantasmagoria ? No ; for we have an internal sense, a sense of our own, which cannot deceive us, which affirms our existence (here is the *Cogito* of Descartes anticipated) and which, at the same time, affirms that there are things which are not ourselves, so that coincidently the ego and the non-ego are established. Yes, but is this non-ego really what it seems ? It is ; granted ; but what is it and can we know what it is ? Not without doubt, and here scepticism is unshakable ; but in that there is certitude of the existence of the non-ego, the presumption is that we can know it, partially, relatively, very relatively, while we remain infinitely distant from an absolute knowledge, which would be divine. Therefore let us observe and experiment; let us make the "history" of nature as historians make the history of the human race. And this is the simple and solid philosophy of experiment.

But Campanella, like so many more, was a metaphysician possessed by the devil of metaphysics, and after having imperiously recommended the writing of only the history of nature, he himself wrote its romance as well. Every being, he said (and the thought was a very fine one), exists on condition of being able to exist, and on condition that there be an idea of which it is the realisation, and again on condition that nature is willing to create it. In other words, nature can, knows what she wishes, and wishes. Now all beings, in a greater or less degree according to their perfection or imperfection, feel this triple condition of being able, knowing and wishing. Every being can, knows and wishes, even inorganic matter (here already is the world as will and representation of Schopenhauer) and God is only absolute power, absolute knowledge, and absolute will. This is why all created things gravitate to

God and desire to return to Him as to their origin, and as the perfection of what they are: the universe has nostalgia for God.

Campanella was also, as we should say nowadays, a sociologist. He made his "Republic" as Plato had made his. The Republic of Campanella was called the *City of the Sun.* It was a community republic, leavened with aristocracy with "spiritual power" and "temporal power" somewhat after the manner of Auguste Comte. Campanella was a great sower of ideas.

Francis Bacon.—Francis Bacon, lawyer, member of Parliament, Lord Chancellor of England, personal friend of James I, friend, protector, and perhaps collaborator of Shakespeare, overthrown as the result of political animosity and relegated to private life, was a very learned man with a marvellous mind. Like his namesake, Roger Bacon, but in an age more favourable to intellectual reform, he attempted a sort of renewal of the human mind (*Instauratio Magna*) or at least a radical revolution in the methods and workings of the human mind. Although Francis Bacon professed admiration for many of the thinkers of antiquity, he urged that it was wrong to rely on them because they had not sufficiently observed; one must not, like the schoolmen, have ideas *a priori*, which are "idols," and there are idols of tribe, of party, of school, of eras; intentions must not be perceived everywhere in nature, and we must not, because the sun warms, believe it was created to warm, or because the earth yields nourishment believe her creation was for the purpose of feeding us, and that all things converge to man and are put at his service. It is necessary to proceed by observation, by experiment, and then by induction, but with prodigious mistrust of induction. Induction consists in drawing conclusions from the particular to the general, from a certain number of facts to a law. This is legitimate on condition that the conclusion is not drawn from a few facts to a law, which is percipitate induction, fruitful in errors; but from a very large number of facts to a law, which even then is considered as provisional. As for metaphysics, as for the investigation of universal law, that should be entirely separated from philosophy itself, from the "primary philosophy" which does not lead to it; it has its own field, which is that of faith: "Give to faith what belongeth to faith." In the main he is uninterested in metaphysics, believing them always to revolve in a circle and, I do not say, only believes in science and in method, but has hope only from knowledge and method, an enthusiast in this respect just as another might be about the supersensible world or about ideas, saying human knowledge and human power are really coincident, and believing that knowledge will support humanity in all calamities, will prolong human life, will establish a new golden age, etc.

Moreover, let there be none of that eternal and unfounded fear that knowledge will cause the disappearance of the religious feeling. With profound conviction and judging by himself, Bacon said: "A little philosophy inclineth a man's mind to atheism, but depth in philosophy bringeth a man's mind about to religion." Such is true philosophy, "subordinate to the object," attentive to the object, listening to the voices of the world and only anxious to translate them into human language: "that is true philosophy which renders the voices of the world the most accurately possible, like an echo, which writes as if at the dictation of the world itself, adding nothing of its own, only repeating and *resounding*."

And, as a man is always of his time, he believed in alchemy and in the possibility of transmuting base metals into gold. But note how he understood it: "To create a new nature in a given body or to produce new natures and to introduce them . . . he who is acquainted with the forms and modes of superinducing yellowness, weight, ductility, fixity, fluidity, solution, and the rest, with their gradations and methods, will see and take care that these properties be united in some body, whence its transformation into gold may follow." Modern chemistry, with scientific methods highly analogous to those which Bacon indicated or foresaw, has not made gold, which is not a very useful thing to do, but has done better.

THOMAS HOBBES.—At the end of the sixteenth century, another Englishman, Thomas Hobbes, began to think. He was, above all else, a literary man and a sociologist; he translated Thucydides and Homer, he wrote *Leviathan, or the Matter, Form and Power of a Commonwealth*, which is a manual of despotism, demonstrating that all men in a natural state were beasts of prey with regard to one another, but that they escaped this unpleasant fate by submission to a prince, who has all rights because he is perpetually saving his subjects from death, and who can therefore impose on them whatever he pleases, even scientific dogma or religious beliefs. Merely regarded as a philosopher properly so called, Hobbes has an important position in the history of ideas. Like Francis Bacon, but more rigorously and authoritatively, he began by separating metaphysics and theology from philosophy. Philosophy is the art of thinking. That which is not sensible—mind, soul, God—cannot be thought: can only be believed; philosophy does not deny all that; merely it does not concern itself therewith. Here is the whole of positivism established in principle. What we can think is what we feel. Things are only known to us through sensations; a thought is a sensation, the human mind is a compound of sensations.

No; for I can think of a thing without hearing, seeing, feeling it, etc.

This is because we have memory, which is itself a sensation; it is a sensation which prolongs itself; to remember is to feel that one has felt; it is to feel a former sensation which the brain is able to preserve. We only think by combining current sensations with other current sensations, or much more often indeed, thanks to memory, by combining current sensations with older ones, or former sensations with each other. This is but a fragile basis for knowledge and thought, for sensation is only a modification of ourselves caused by an external object, and consequently gives us nothing at all of the external object, and of itself the external world is eternally unknown to us; but we combine with each other the illusions that the external world deposits in us through the delusive or doubtful intermediary of our senses.

When the sensation thus combined with other sensations has become thought, then ideas begin to exist. They are products of sensation detached from sensation. They are inter-associated by laws that are obscure, yet which can be vaguely perceived. They awake, so to speak, and call to one another; every time an idea previously acquired reappears, it is followed by the thought which accompanied it when it was acquired. In a conversation a traitor is spoken of. Someone asks what was the value of a piece of silver in ancient times. This appears incoherent; really it is a natural and simple association of ideas in which there are few intermediate steps. The person who listened as the traitor was mentioned thought of Judas, who was the first traitor of whom he had heard, and of the thirty pieces of silver, the price of the betrayal by Judas. The association of ideas is more or less close, more or less loose; it is disconnected in dreams, irregular in musing, close directly it is dominated and in consequence directed by an end pursued, by a goal sought; for then there is a desire to attain which associates nothing of itself, but which, eliminating all ideas that are not pertinent to the end pursued, only permits the association of those which have relation to it.

Only seeing in the human soul successive

impulses arising from those first impulses which are the sensations, Hobbes does not believe we are free to do what we wish; we are carried away by the strongest impulse of our internal impulses, desire, fear, aversion, love, etc. Nevertheless we deliberate, we consider different courses to pursue and we decide on the one we desire to choose. No; we do not deliberate, we only imagine we deliberate. Deliberation is only a succession of different feelings, and to the one that gains the day we give the name of volition. "In the [so-called] deliberation, the final desire or the final fear is called will." Therefore liberty has no more existence among men than among animals; will and desire are only one and the same thing considered under different aspects.

Utilitarian Morality.—Henceforth there is no morality; without the power to will this and not to will that, there is no possible morality. Hobbes retorts with "utilitarian morality": What man should seek is pleasure, as Aristippus thought; but true pleasure—that which is permanent and that which is useful to him. Now it is useful to be a good citizen, a loyal subject, sociable, serviceable to others, careful to obtain their esteem by good conduct, etc. Morality is interest rightly understood, and interest rightly understood is absolutely blended with the morality of duty. The criminal is not a criminal but an idiot; the honest man is not an honest man but an intelligent one. Observe that a man is hardly convinced when preached to in the name of duty, but always convinced when addressed in the name of his own interest.

All this is fairly sensible; but from the time that freedom ceases there can be no morality, *not even utilitarian;* for it is useless even from the point of view of his own interests, to preach to a man who is only a machine moved by the strongest force; and, if he be only that, to lay down a moral code for him either from the point of view of his own interests, or from that of morality, or from that of the love of God are things which are the same and which are as absurd the one as the other. All philosophy, which does not believe in human liberty, yet which enunciates a system of morality, is in perpetual contradiction.

Part III.

MODERN TIMES.

CHAPTER I.

THE SEVENTEENTH CENTURY.

Descartes. Cartesianism.

DESCARTES.—The seventeenth century, which was the greatest philosophic century of modern times and perhaps of any time, began with René Descartes. Descartes, born at La Haye in Touraine in 1596, of noble family (his real name was des Quartes), was educated by the Jesuits of the college of La Flèche, followed the military profession for several years, then gave himself up to mathematics and became one of the greatest mathematicians of Europe, travelled all over Europe for his own amusement and instruction, wrote scientific and philosophical works, of which the most famous are the *Discourse on Method*, the *Meditations* and the *Rules for the Control of the Mind*, resided sometimes at Paris, sometimes in Holland and finally, at fifty-four years of age, unhappily attracted by the flattering invitations of Queen Christina of Sweden, proceeded to Stockholm, where he succumbed in four months to the severity of the climate. He died in February, 1650.

THE SYSTEM OF DESCARTES.—In the works of

Descartes there are a general system of philosophy, a psychology, and a method. This order is here adopted because of the three, in Descartes, it is the third which is the most important, and which has left the most profound traces. The foundation of the system of Descartes is belief in God and in the goodness of God. I say the foundation and not the starting-point. The starting-point is another matter; but it will be clearly seen that the foundation is what has just been stated. The starting-point is this: I do not believe, provisionally, in anything, not wishing to take into account what I have been taught. I doubt everything. Is there anything I cannot doubt? It seems to me there is; I cannot doubt that I doubt. Now if I doubt, I think; if I think, I am. There is one certainty, I am.

And having arrived there, Descartes is at a dead stop, for from the certitude of one's own existence nothing can be deduced save the certitude of one's existence. For instance, shall I believe in the existence of everything that is not myself? There is no reason why I should believe in it. The world may be a dream. But if I believe in God and in a God of perfect goodness, I can then believe in something outside of myself, for God not being able to deceive Himself or me, if He permits me to see the external world, it is because this external world exists. There are already, therefore, three things in which I believe: my own existence, that of God, and that of the universe. Which of these beliefs is the fundamental one? Evidently, the one not demonstrated; the axiom is that upon which one rests to demonstrate everything except itself. Now of the three things in which Descartes believed, his own existence is demonstrated by the impossibility of thinking or feeling, without feeling his own existence; the other is demonstrated by the existence of a good God; the existence of a good God is demonstrated by nothing. It is believed. Hence belief in a good God is Descartes' foundation. This has not been introduced in order that he may escape from the *I am* at which he came to a stop; that belief certainly existed previously, and if he had recourse to it, it was because it existed first. Without that, he had too much intellectual honesty to invent it for a particular need. He had it, and he found it as it were in reserve when he asked himself if he could go beyond *I am.* Here was his foundation; all the rest would complete the proof.

THE EXISTENCE OF GOD.—Although Descartes rests on God as being his first principle, he does not fail to prove His existence, and that is begging the question, something proved by what has to be proved. For if Descartes only believed in something outside himself because of a good God, that Being outside himself, God, he can only prove because of the existence of a good God, Who cannot deceive us, and thus is God proved by the belief in Him. That is begging the question. Descartes does not fail to prove the existence of God by superabundance as it were; and this, too, in itself indicates clearly that faith in God is the very foundation of the philosophy of Descartes. After having taken it as the basis of reasoning, he takes it as the goal of reasoning, which indicates that the idea of God, so to speak, encircled his mind and that he found it at every ultimate point of thought.

He proves it, therefore, first by an argument analogous to that of St. Anselm, which is this : we, imperfect and finite, have the idea of a perfect and infinite Being; we are not capable of this idea. Therefore it must have come to us from a Being really perfect and infinite, and hence this perfect Being exists.

Another proof, that of God regarded as cause. First : I exist. Who made me ? Was it myself ? No, if it had been myself I should have endowed myself with all the perfections which I can conceive and in which I am singularly deficient.

Therefore it must be some other being who created me. It was my parents. No doubt, but who created my parents and the parents of my parents ? One cannot go back indefinitely from cause to cause, and there must have been a first one.

Secondly : even my own actual existence, my existence at this very moment, is it the result of my existence yesterday ? Nothing proves it, and there is no necessity because I existed just now that I should exist at present. There must therefore be a cause at each moment and a continuous cause. That continuous cause is God, and the whole world is a creation perpetually continued, and is only comprehensible as continuous creation and is only explicable by a Creator.

The World.—Thus sure of himself, of God and of the world, Descartes studies the world and himself. In the world he sees souls and matter ; matter is substance in extension, souls are substance not in extension, spiritual substance. The extended substance is endowed with impulse Is the impulse self-generated, are the bodies self-impelled ? No, they are moved. What is the primary motive force ? It is God. Souls are substances without extension and motive forces. In this respect they are analogous to God. They are united to bodies and act on them. How? This is an impenetrable mystery, but they are closely and substantially united to the bodies, which is proved by physical pains depressing the soul and moral sufferings depressing the body; and they act on them, not by creating movements, for the quantity of movements is always the same, but by directing the movements after this fashion or that. Souls being spiritual, there is no reason for their disaggregation, that is their demise, and in fact they do not die.

It is for this reason that Descartes lays such stress on animals not having souls. If they had souls, the souls would be spiritual, they would not be susceptible to disaggregation and would be immortal. "Save atheism, there is no doctrine more dangerous and detestable than that," but animals are soulless and purely mechanism; Descartes exerts himself to prove this in great detail, and he thus escapes avowing the immortality of the souls of animals, which is repugnant to him, or by allowing that they perish with the bodies to be exposed to the objection: "will it not be the same with the souls of men?"

The Freedom of the Soul.—This human soul is endowed with freedom to do good or evil. What proof is there of this freedom? First, the inward feeling that we have. Every evident idea is true. Now, not only have we the idea of this freedom, but it would be impossible for us not to have it. Freedom "is known without proofs, merely by the experience we have of it." It is by the feeling of our freedom, of our free-will that we understand that we exist as a being, as a thing which is not merely a thing. The true *ego* is the will. Even more than an intelligent being, man is a free individual, and only feels himself to be a man when feeling himself free, so that he might not believe himself to be intelligent, nor think himself sensible, etc., but not to think himself free would for him be moral suicide; and in fact he actually never does anything which he does not believe himself to be free to do, that is which he does not believe that he might avoid doing, if he so wished. Those who say "it is simply the feeling that it is better for ourselves which tends to make us do this instead of doing that," are deeply in error. They forget that we often prefer the worst for ourselves in order to prove to ourselves that we are free and therefore have no other *motive power than our own freedom*. (And this is exactly what contemporaneous philosophy has thus formulated: "will is neither determinate nor indeterminate, it is determinative.") "Even when a very obvious reason leads us to a thing, although morally speaking it is difficult for us to do the opposite, nevertheless, speaking absolutely, we can, for we are always free to prevent ourselves from pursuing a good thing clearly known . . . provided only that *we think it is beneficial thereby to give evidence of the truth of our free-will.*" It is the pure and simple wish to be free which *creates an action;* it is the all-powerful liberty.

As has been happily observed, in relation to the universe the philosophy of Descartes is a mechanical philosophy; in relation to man the philosophy of Descartes is a philosophy of will. As has also been remarked, there are very striking analogies between Corneille and Descartes from the point of view of the apotheosis of the will, and the *Meditations* having appeared after the great works of Corneille, it is not so much that Corneille was a Cartesian, as that Descartes was a follower of Corneille.

PSYCHOLOGY OF DESCARTES.—Descartes has almost written a psychology, what with his *Treatise on the Passions* and his letters and besides certain passages in his *Meditations.* The soul thinks and has passions. There are three kinds of ideas, the factitious, the adventitious and the innate; the factitious ideas are those which the imagination forms; the adventitious ideas are those suggested by the external world through the intermediary of the senses ; the innate ideas are those constituting the mind itself, the conditions under which it thinks and apart from which it cannot think : we cannot conceive an object not extended, nor an object apart from time, nor anything without a cause ; the ideas of time, space, and cause are innate ideas ; we cannot conceive ourselves as other than free, the idea of liberty is an innate idea.

The soul has passions ; it is therein that, without dependence on the body, it has intimate relations with and is modified by it, not radically, but in its daily life. There are operations of the soul which cannot strictly be termed passions, and yet which are directed or at least *influenced* by the body. Memory is passive, and consequently memory is a species of passion. The lively sensations which the body transmits to the brain leave impressions (Malebranche would say : " traces "), and according to these impressions the soul is moved a second or a third time, and that is what is called memory. " The impressions of the brain render it suitable to stir the soul in the same way as it has been stirred before, and also to make it recollect something, just as the folds in a piece of paper or linen make it more suitable to be folded anew as it was before than if it had never been thus folded." Similarly, the association of ideas is passive, and in consequence is a kind of passion. The association of ideas is the fact that thought passes along the same path it has already traversed, and follows in its labyrinth the thread which interlinks its thoughts, and this thread is the traces which thoughts have left in the brain. In abandoning ourselves to the association of ideas, we are passive and we yield ourselves freely to a passion. That is so true that current speech itself recognises this : musing is a passion, it is possible to have a passion for musing, and musing is nothing else than the association of ideas in which the will does not intervene.

THE PASSIONS.—Coming to the passions strictly speaking, there are some which are of the soul and only of the soul ; the passion for God is a passion of the soul, the passion for liberty is a passion of the soul ; but there are many more which are the effects of the union of the soul with the body. These passions are excited in the soul by a state of the body or a movement of the body or of some part of the body ; they are "emotions" of the soul corresponding to "movements" of the machine. All passions have relation to the desire of pleasure and the fear of pain, and according as they relate to the former or the latter are they expansive or oppressive. There are six principal passions, of which all the rest are only modifications : admiration, love, desire, joy having relation to the appetite of happiness, hatred, sadness having relation to the fear o pain. " All the passions are good and may become bad " (Descartes in this deviates emphatically from Stoicism for which the passions are simply maladies of the soul). All passions are good in themselves. They are destined (this is a remarkable theory) to cause the duration of thoughts which would otherwise pass and be rapidly effaced ; by reason of this, they cause man to act ; if he were only directed by his thoughts, unaccompanied by his passions, he would never act, and if it be recognised that man is born for action, it will at the same time be recognised that it is necessary he should have passions.

But, you will say, there can be good passions (of a nature to give force to just ideas) and evil passions.

No, they are all good, but all also have their bad side, their deviation, rather, which enables them to become bad. Therefore, in each passion no matter what it be, it is always possible to distinguish between the passion itself, which is always good, and the excess, the deviation, the degradation or corruption of this passion which constitutes, if it be desired to call it so, an evil passion, and this is what Descartes demonstrates, passion by passion, in the fullest detail, in his *Treatise on the Passions.*

THE PART OF THE SOUL.—If it is thus, what will be the part of the soul (the soul is the will)? It will be to abandon itself to good passions, or more accurately to the good that is in all passions, and to reduce the passions to be "nothing more than themselves." In courage, for example, there is courage and temerity. The action of the will, enlightened by the judgment, will consist in reducing courage to be nothing but courage. In fear, there is cowardice and there is the feeling of self-preservation which, according to Descartes, is the foundation of fear and which is a very good passion. The action of the soul is to reduce fear to simple prudence.

But *how* will the will effect these metamorphoses or at least these departures, these separations, these reductions to the due proportion? *Directly* it can effect *nothing* upon the passions; it cannot *remove* them; it cannot even remove the baser portions of them; but it can exercise influence over them by the intermediary of reasoning; it can lead them to the attentive consideration of the thought that they carry with them, and by this consideration modify them.

For instance, if it is a question of fear, the soul forces fear to consider that the peril is much less than was imagined, and thus little by little brings it back to simple prudence.

Note that this method, although indirect, is very potent; for it ends by really transforming the passions into their opposites. Persuade fear that there is less peril in marching forward than in flight and that the most salutary flight is the flight forward and you have changed fear to courage.—But such an influence of the will over the passions is extraordinarily unlikely: it will never take place.—Yes, by habit! Habit too is a passion, or if you will a passive state, like that of memory or the association of ideas, and there are men possessed only of that passion. But the will, by the means which have been described, by imposing an act, a first act, creates a commencement of habit, by imposing a second confirms that habit, by imposing a third strengthens it, and so on. In plain words, the will, by reasoning with the passions and reasoning with them incessantly, brings them back to what is good in them and ends by bringing them back there permanently, so that it arrives at having only the passions it desires, or, if you prefer it, for it is the same thing, at having only the passion for good. Morality consists in loving noble passions, as was later observed by Vauvenargues, and that means to love all the passions, each for what is good in it, that is to reduce each passion to what real goodness is inherent in it, and that is to gather all the passions into one, which is the passion of duty.

THE METHOD OF DESCARTES.—As has been observed, not only had Descartes influence through all that he wrote, but it was by his method that he has exerted the greatest and most durable sway, and that is why we conclude with the examination of his method. It is all contained in this : to accept nothing as true except what is evident ; to accept as true all that is evident. Descartes therefore made evidence the touchstone of certainty. But mark well the profound meaning of this method : what is it that gives me the assurance of the evidence of such or such an idea ? How shall I know that such an idea is really evident to me ? Because I see it in perfect clearness ? No, that does not suffice : the evidence may be deceptive ; there can be false evidence ; all the wrong ideas of the philosophers of antiquity, save when they were sophists, had for them the character of being evident. Why ? Why should error be presented to the mind as an evident truth ? Because in truth, in profound truthfulness, it must be admitted that judgment does not depend upon the intelligence. And on what does it depend? On will, on free-will. This is how. No doubt, error depends on our judgment, but our judgment depends on our will in the sense that it depends on us whether we adhere to our judgment without it being sufficiently precise or do not adhere to it because it is not sufficiently precise: "If I abstain from giving my judgment on a subject when I do not conceive it with sufficient clearness and distinction, it is evident that I shall not be deceived." Evidence is therefore not only a matter of judgment, of understanding, of intelligence, it is a matter of energetic will and of freedom courageously acquired. We are confronted with evidence when, with a clear brain, we are capable, in order to accept or refuse what it lays before us, of acting "after such a fashion," of having put ourselves in such a state of the soul that we feel "that no external force can constrain us to think in such or such a way."

These external forces are authority, prejudices, personal interest, or that of party. The faculty of perceiving evidence is therefore the triumph both of sound judgment in itself and of a freedom of mind which, supposing probity, scrupulousness and courage, and perhaps the most difficult of all courage, supposes a profound and vigorous morality. Evidence is only given to men who are first highly intelligent and next, or rather before all else, are profoundly honest. Evidence is not a consequence of morality; but morality is the *condition* of evidence.

There is the foundation of the Method of Descartes; add to it his advice on the art of reasoning, which even in his time was not at all novel, but which with him is very precise; not to generalise too hastily, not to be put off with words, but to have a clear definition of every word, etc., and thus a sufficient idea of it will be obtained.

Now first, to this method Descartes was unfaithful, as always happens, and often accepted the suggestions of his magnificent imàgination as the evidences of his reason; secondly, the touchstone of evidence is certainly the best, but is far from being infallible (and Vico has ridiculed it with as much sense as wit) and the freest mind can still find false things evident; yet, thirdly, favouring freedom of research self-controlled, individual and scornful of all authority, the method of Descartes has become a banner, a motto and a flag for all modern philosophy.

Descartes the Father of Modern Philosophy.—And from all that the result has been that all modern philosophy, with few exceptions, has recognised Descartes as its parent—that individual evidence, if it may be thus expressed, favouring temerity and each believing himself closer to the truth the more he differed from others, and consequently was unable to suspect himself of being subject to influences, individual evidence has provided a fresh opportunity for self-deception; finally, that Descartes, by a not uncommon metamorphosis, by means of his system which he did not follow, has become the head or the venerated ancestor of doctrines which he would have detested and which he already did detest more than all others. Because he said that evidence alone and the free investigation of evidence led to truth, he has become the ancestor of the sceptics who are persuaded that surrender must only be made to evidence and that evidence cannot be found; and he has become the ancestor of the positivists who believe that evidence certainly exists somewhere, but not in metaphysics or in theodicy, or in knowledge of the soul, of immortality, and of God, branches of knowledge which surpass our means of knowing, which are in fact outside knowledge. So that this man who conceived more than any man, this man who so often constructed without a sure foundation, and this man, yet again, as has been aptly said, who always thought by innate ideas, by his formula has become the master and above all the guarantor of those who are the most reserved and most distrustful as to philosophic construction, innate ideas, and imagination. This does not in the least diminish his brilliant merit ; it is only one of those changes of direction in which the history of ideas abounds.

CHAPTER II.

CARTESIANS.

All the Seventeenth Century was under the Influence of Descartes. Port-Royal, Bossuet, Fénelon. Malebranche, Spinoza, Leibnitz.

CARTESIAN INFLUENCE.—Nearly all the seventeenth century was Cartesian, and in the general sense of the word, not only as supporters of the method of evidence, but as adherents of the general philosophy of Descartes. Gassendi (a Provençal, and not an Italian), professor of philosophy at Aix, subsequently in Paris, was not precisely a faithful disciple of Descartes, and he opposed him several times; he had leanings towards Epicurus and the doctrine of atoms; he drew towards Hobbes, but he was also a fervent admirer of Bacon, and so approached Descartes, who thought very highly of him, though impatiently galled by his criticisms. After the example of Epicurus he was the most sober and austere of men, and of the two it was Descartes rather than he who was Epicurean in the common use of the word. According to a tradition, which to my mind rests on insufficient proof, he was an instructor of Molière.

All the thinkers of the seventeenth century

came more or less profoundly under the Cartesian influence: Pascal, Bossuet, Fénelon, Arnauld, and all Port-Royal. This influence was only to diminish in the eighteenth century, though kept up by the impenitent Fontenelle, but outweighed by that of Locke, to reappear very vigorously in the nineteenth century in France in the school of Maine de Biran and of Cousin.

MALEBRANCHE.—A separate niche must be made for the Cartesians, almost as great as Descartes, who filled the seventeenth century with their renown, the Frenchman, Malebranche, the Dutchman, Spinoza, and the German, Leibnitz. Pushing the theories of Descartes further than Descartes would himself in all probability have desired to, from what Descartes had said that it was only *through God* that we perceived accurately, Malebranche declared that it was only *in God* that we perceived accurately, and fundamentally this is the same idea; it can only be deemed that Malebranche is the more precise: "God alone is known by Himself [is believed in without uncertainty]; there is only He that we can see in immediate and direct perspective." All the rest we see in Him, in His light, in the light He creates in our minds. When we see, it is that we are in Him. Evidence is divine light. He is the link of ideas. (And thus Malebranche brought

Plato near to Descartes and showed that, without the latter being aware of it, they both said the same thing). God is always the cause and as He is the cause of all real things, He is cause also of all truths, and as He is everywhere in real objects, He is also everywhere in the true ideas which we can have, or rather in which we can participate. When we seek a truth we pray without thinking we do so; attention is a prayer.

In the same way, from the saying of Descartes that the universe is a continuous creation, Malebranche deduced or rather concluded that our thoughts and actions are acts of God. There can be no action of the body on the soul to produce ideas; that would be inconceivable; but on the occasion, for instance, of our eyes resting on an object, God gives us an idea of that object, whether in conformity or not we cannot tell; but at any rate He gives us that idea of the object which He wishes us to have.

There is no action of our soul on our body; that would be inconceivable. But God to our will adds a force having a tendency towards goodness as a rule, and to each of our volitions adds a force tending to its execution and capable of executing it.

Then, when our will is evil and we execute it, does God sin in our name?

Certainly not; because sin is not an act; it consists in doing nothing, it consists precisely in the soul not acting on the body; therefore it is not a force but a weakness. Sin is that God has withdrawn himself from us. The sinner is only a being who is without strength because he is lacking in grace.

The principle of morality is the respect for order and the love of order. That makes two degrees, the first of which is regularity and the second virtue. To conform to order is highly rational but without merit (*e.g.*, to give money to the poor from habit or possibly from vanity). To love order and to desire that it should be greater, more complete, and nearer to the will of God, is to adhere to God, to live in God, just as to see rightly is to see in God. All morality, into the details of which we will not enter, evolves from the love of order. The universe is a vast mechanism, as was stated by Descartes, set in motion and directed by God, that is to say by the laws established by God; for God only acts by general dispositions (which are laws) and not by particular dispositions. In other words, there exists a will, but there are no volitions.

MIRACLES.—But then you will say there are no miracles; for miracle is precisely a particular will traversing and interrupting the general will.

To begin with, there are very few miracles, which therefore permits order to subsist; it would be only if there were incessant miracles that order would be non-existent. Next, a miracle is a warning God gives to men because of their weakness, to remind them that behind the laws there is a Law-giver, behind the general dispositions a Being who disposes. Because of their intellectual weakness, if they never saw any derogation from the general laws they would take them to be fatalities. A miracle is a grace intervening in things, just as grace properly so-called intervenes in human actions. And it is not contradictory to the general design of God, since by bringing human minds back to the truth that thereis a Being who wills, it accustoms them to consider all general laws as permanent acts, but also as the acts of the Being who wills. The miracle has the virtue of making everything in the world miraculous, which is true. Hence the miracle confirms the idea of order. Therein, perhaps alone, the exception proves the rule.

Spinoza.—Spinoza, who during his life was a pure Stoic and the purest of Stoics, polishing the lenses of astronomical telescopes in order to gain his living, refusing all pensions and all the professorial positions offered to him, and living well-nigh on nothing, had read Descartes and to conform to the principle of evidence, had begun by renouncing his religion which was that of the Jews. His general outlook on the world was this: There is only one God. God is all. Only He has His attributes, that is to say, His manners of being and His modes, that is His modifications, as the sun (merely a comparison) has as its manners of being, its roundness, colour, and heat, as modifications its rays, terrestial heat, direct and diffused light, etc. Now God has two attributes, thought and extension, as had already been observed by Descartes; and for modifications He has exactly all we can see, touch, or feel, etc. The human soul is an attribute of God, as is everything else; it is an attribute of God in His power. It is not free, for all that comes from God, all that *is of God*, is a regular and necessary development of God Himself. " There is nothing contingent " [nothing which may either happen or not happen]. All things are determined, by the necessity of the divine nature, to exist and to act in a given manner. There is therefore no free-will in the soul, the soul is determined to will this or that by a cause which is itself determined by another and that by another, and so on to infinity.

Nevertheless we believe ourselves to be free and according to the principle of evidence we are;

for nothing is more evident to us than our liberty. We are as intimately convinced of our liberty as of our existence and we *all* affirm, I am free,—with the same emphasis that Descartes affirms: I am. I am and I am free are the two things it is impossible for man to doubt, no matter what effort he makes.

No doubt, but it is an illusion. It is the illusion of a being who feels himself as cause, but does not feel himself as effect. Try to imagine a billiard ball which feels it moves others, but which does not feel that it is moved. What we call decision is an idea which decides us because it exercises more power over us than the others do; what we term deliberation is a hesitancy between two or three ideas which at the moment have equal force; what we name volition is an idea, and what we call will is our understanding applied to facts. We do not want to fight; we conceive the idea of fighting and the idea carries us away; we do not want to hang ourselves; we have the obsessing idea of hanging ourselves and this thought runs away with us.

His Moral System.—Spinoza wrote a system of morality. Is it not radically impossible to write a system of morality when the author does not believe in free-will? The admirable originality of Spinoza, even though his idea can be contested, is precisely that morality depends on belief in the necessity of all things, that is the more one is convinced of this necessity so much the more does one attain high morality, that is the more one believes oneself free the more one is *immoral.* The man who believes himself free claims to run counter to the universal order, and morality precisely is adherence to it ; the man who believes himself free seeks for an individual good just as if there could be an individual good, just as if the best for each one were not to submit to the necessary laws of everything, laws which constitute what is good ; the man who thinks himself free sets himself against God, believes himself God since he believes himself to be creator of what he does and since he believes himself capable of deranging something in the mechanism and of introducing a certain amount of movement. As a matter of fact, he does nothing of the kind ; but he believes that he does it, and this mere thought, false and low as it is, keeps him in the most miserable condition of life ; to sum up, a man who believes himself free may not perhaps be an atheist, but he is ungodly.

On the contrary, the man who does not believe himself free believes he is in the hands of God, and that is the beginning of wisdom and the beginning of virtue. We are in the hands of God as the clay is in those of the potter; the mad vase would be the one which reproached the potter for having made it small instead of big, common instead of decorative. It is the beginning of wisdom to believe oneself in the hands of God; to see Him, to see Him the least indistinctly that we can, therein lies the highest wisdom; we must see His designs, or at least His great design and associate ourselves with it, thus becoming not only part of Him, which we always are, but a conscient part of Him.

This is the love of God, and the love of God is virtue itself. We ought to love God without consideration of the good He can do us and of the penalties He can inflict upon us; for to love God from love of a beneficent God or from fear of a punitive God is not to love God but to love oneself.

THE PASSIONS.—We have our passions as enemies and as obstacles to our elevation to this semi-perfection. It is they which cause us to do immoral acts. "Immoral," has that a meaning from the moment that we do nothing which we are not obliged to do? Yes, just as when led by our deceitful mind we have arrived necessarily at a false idea, the fact of this thought being necessary does not prevent it from being false; we may have been led by necessity to commit a villainous action, but that does not prevent its being immoral. The passions are our imperfections, omissions, gaps in a soul which is not full of the idea of God and of universal order and the love of God and of universal order, and which in consequence, lives individually, that is, separated from the universe.

The passions are infinite in number and Spinoza, in a bulky volume, furnished a minute and singularly profound description of the principal ones alone, into the details of which we regret that we cannot enter. The *Ethic* of Spinoza is an incomparable masterpiece.

The study of the passions is very salutary, because in studying them one gets so detached from them that one can perceive their emptiness, their meanness, and their puerile, nay, even bestial character. It might even be added that the mere thought of studying them is already an act of detachment in reference to them. "Thou wouldst not seek Me, hadst thou not already found Me," said God to Pascal. "Thou wouldst not make investigations about us hadst thou not already quitted us," the passions might say to the philosopher.

Sanctions of Morality.—What are the sanctions of morality? They are necessary sanctions; just as everything is necessary and may even be said to be mechanical. There is neither merit nor demerit and the criminal is not culpable; only he is outside order, and everything must be in order. "He who is maddened by the bite of a mad dog is certainly innocent; yet anyone has the right to suffocate him. In the same way, the man who cannot govern his passions by fear of the law is a very excusable invalid; yet he cannot enjoy peace of mind, nor the knowledge of God nor yet the love of God, and it is necesssary that he perish." Through death he has re-entered within order.

But does the sanction of beyond-the-grave exist and is the soul immortal and are we to be rewarded therein in another life? The conclusion of Spinoza on this matter is hesitating, but at the risk of misrepresenting it, which I fear to do, it seems to me that it can be thus summed up—*The soul makes itself immortal;* in proportion as by the knowledge and love of God it participates more in God. In proportion it makes itself divine; and approaching perfection, by the same progress it also approaches immortality. It is conceivable that by error and sin it kills itself, and by virtue renders itself imperishable. This immortality is not or does not seem to be personal, it is literally a definite re-entry into the bosom of God; Spinozian immortality would therefore be a prolongation of the same effort which we make in this life to adhere to universal order; the recompense for having adhered to it here below is to be absorbed in it there, and in that lies true beatitude. Here below we ought to see everything from the point of view of eternity (*sub specie aeternitatis*) and this is a way of being eternal; elsewhere we shall be in eternity itself.

LEIBNITZ.—Leibnitz possessed a universal mind, being historian, naturalist, politician, diplomatist, scholar, theologian, mathematician; here we will only regard him as philosopher. For Leibnitz the basis, the substance of all beings is not either thought or extension as with Descartes, but is force, productive of action. "What does not act does not exist." Everything that exists is a force, either action or tendency to action. And force, all force has two characteristics: it desires to do, it wishes to think. The world is the graduated compound of all these forces. Above all there is the supreme force, God, Who is infinite force, infinite thought; by successive descents those base and obscure forces are reached which seem to have neither power nor thought, and yet have a minimum of power and even of thought, so to speak, latent. God thinks and acts infinitely; man thinks and acts powerfully, thanks to reason, which distinguishes him from the rest of creation;

the animal acts and thinks dimly, but it does act and think, for it has a soul composed of memory and of the results and consequences of memory, and by parenthesis " three-fourths of our own actions are governed by memory, and most frequently we act like animals " ; plants act, and if they do not think, at least feel (which is still thought) though more dimly than animals ; and finally in the mineral kingdom the power of action and thought slumber, but are not non-existent since they can be transformed into plants, animals, and men, into living matter which feels and thinks.

Therefore, as was later on to be maintained by Schopenhauer, everything is full of souls, and of souls which are forces as well as intelligences. The human soul is a force too, like the body. Between these two forces, which seem to act on one another and which certainly act in concert in such fashion that the movement desired by the soul is executed by the body or that the soul obviously assents to a movement desired by the body, what can be the affinity and the relation, in what consists their concurrence and concord ? Leibnitz (and there was already something of the same nature suggested by Descartes), believes that all the forces of the world act, each spontaneously ; but that among all the actions they perform there exists an agreement imposed by

God, a concord establishing universal order, a "pre-established harmony" causing them all to co-operate in the same design. Well, then, between the soul, this force, and the body, this force also, this harmony reigns as between any force whatever in nature and one and all of the rest; and that is the explanation of the union and concord between the soul and the body. Imagine two well-constructed clocks wound up by the same maker; they indicate the same hour, and it might appear that this one directs the other, or that the other directs the first. All the forces of the world are clocks which agree with each other, because they have been regulated in advance by the divine clock-maker, and they all indicate the eternal hour.

THE RADICAL OPTIMISM OF LEIBNITZ.—From all these general views on matter, on mind and on the mind, Leibnitz arrived at a radical optimism which is the thing for which he has since been most ridiculed, and by which, at any rate, he has remained famous. He believes that all is good, despite the evil of which no one can dispute the existence; and he believes that all is the best *possible* in the best of *possible* worlds. In fact, God is supreme wisdom and supreme goodness, that was quite evident to Descartes, who in the matter of evidence was not easily satisfied. This perfect wisdom and perfect goodness could only choose what is best.—But yet evil exists! Diminish it as much as you choose, it still exists.—It exists by a necessity inherent in what is created. Everything created is imperfect. God alone is perfect; what is imperfect is by its definition evil mingled with good. Evil is only the boundary of good, where God was compelled to stop in creating beings and things other than Himself, and if He had only created according to absolute goodness, He could only have created Himself. And that is the precise meaning of this phrase "the best of possible worlds"; the world is perfect so far as that which is created, and therefore imperfect, can be perfect; so far as what is not God can be divine; the world is God himself as far as He can remain Himself whilst being anything else than Himself.

The Three Evils.—Let us distinguish in order to comprehend better. There are three evils; the metaphysical, the physical, and the moral. Metaphysical evil is this very fact of not being perfection; it is natural enough that what only emanates from perfection should not be perfection. Physical evil is suffering; God cannot *will* suffering, desire it, or cherish it; but He can permit it as a means of good, as a condition of good; for there would be no moral good if there were not occasion for struggle, and there would be no occasion for struggling if physical evil did not exist: imagine a paradise; all the inhabitants merely exist and never have cause to show the slightest endurance, the least courage, the smallest virtue. And finally, as to moral evil, which is sin, God can even less desire that it should exist, but He can admit its existence, *allow it to be*, to afford men occasion for merit or demerit. Nothing is more easy than to criticise God whilst only considering a portion of His work and not considering it as a whole. He must have created it to be a whole and it is as a whole that it must be judged. And precisely because the whole cannot be comprehended by anyone, "hold thy peace, foolish reason," as Pascal said, and judge not or judge *a priori*, since here it is not possible to judge by experience; and declare that the Perfect can only have willed the most perfect that is possible.

THE POSSIBLE AND THE IMPOSSIBLE.—There still remains the fundamental objection; to reduce God to the conditions of the *possible* is to limit Him, and it is useless to say that God is justified if He has done all the good possible. He is not; the words "possible" and "impossible" having no meaning to Him who is omnipotent, and by definition infinite power could effect the impossible.

CHAPTER III.

THE ENGLISH PHILOSOPHERS OF THE SEVENTEENTH CENTURY.

Locke: His Ideas on Human Liberty, Morality, General Politics, and Religious Politics.

LOCKE.—Locke, very learned in various sciences, physics, chemistry, medicine, often associated with politics, receiving enlightenment from life, from frequent travels, from friendships with interesting and illustrious men, always studying and reflecting until an advanced old age, wrote only carefully premeditated works; his *Treatise of Government* and *Essay On the Human Understanding.*

Locke appears only to have written on the understanding in order to refute the "innate ideas" of Descartes. For Locke innate ideas have no existence. The mind before it comes into contact with the external world is a blank sheet, and there is nothing in the mind which has not first come through the senses. What, then, are ideas? They are sensations registered by the brain, and they are also sensations elaborated and modified by reflection. These ideas then commingle in such a manner as to form an enormous mass of combinations. They are commingled

Yes, Leibnitz replies, there is a metaphysical impossibility, there is an impossibility in the infinite; this impossibility is absurdity, is contradiction. Could God make the whole smaller than the part or any line shorter than a straight one? Reason replies in the negative. Is God therefore limited? He is limited by the absurd and that means He is unlimited; for the absurd is a falling away. It is therefore credible that the mixture of evil and good is a metaphysical necessity, to which I will not say God submits, but in which He acts naturally, and that the absence of evil is a metaphysical contradiction, an absurdity in itself, which God cannot commit precisely because He is perfect; and no doubt, instead of drawing this conclusion, we should actually see it, were the totality of things, of their relations, of their concordance, and of their harmony known to us.

The optimism of Leibnitz was ridiculed specially in the *Candide* of Voltaire, ingeniously defended by Rousseau, magnificently defended by Victor Hugo in the following verses, well worthy of Leibnitz :—

“ Oui peut-être au delà de la sphère des nues,
Au sein de cet azur immobile et dormant,
Peut-être faites-vous des choses inconnues
Où la douleur de l'homme entre comme élément.”

either in a natural or an artificial manner. In a natural manner, that is in a way conforming to the great primary ideas given us by reflection, the idea of cause, the idea of end, the idea of means to an end, the idea of order, etc., and it is the harmony of these ideas which is commonly termed reason; they become associated by accident, by the effects of emotion, by the effect of custom, etc., and then they give birth to prejudices, errors, and superstitions. The passions of the soul are aspects of pleasure and pain. The idea of a possible pleasure gives birth in us to a desire which is called ambition, love, covetousness, gluttony; the idea of a possible pain gives birth in us to fear and horror, and this fear and horror is called hatred, jealousy, rage, aversion, disgust, scorn. At bottom we have only two passions, the desire of enjoyment, and the fear of suffering.

The Freedom of Man.—Is man free? Appealing to experience and making use only of it and not of intimate feeling, Locke declares in the negative. A will always seems to him determined by another will, and this other by another to infinity, or by a motive, a weight, a motive power which causes a leaning to right or left. Will certainly exists, that is to say, an exact and lively desire to perform an action, or to continue an action, or to interrupt an action, but this will is not free, for to represent it as free is to represent it as capable of wishing what it does not wish. The will is an anxiety to act in such or such a fashion and this anxiety, on account of its character of anxiety, of strong emotion, of tension of the soul, appears to us free, appears to us an internal force which is self-governed and independent; we feel consciousness of will in the effort. This tension must not be denied, but it must be recognised as the effect of a potent desire which the obstacle excites; this tension, therefore, is an indication of nothing except the potency of the desire and the existence of an obstacle. Now this desire, so potent that it is irritated by the obstacle, and, so to speak, unites us against it, is a passion dominating and filling our being; so that we are never more swayed by passion than when we believe ourselves to be exercising our will, and in consequence the more we desire the less are we free.

It is not essential formally and absolutely to confound will with desire. Overpowered by heat, we desire to drink cold water and because we know that that would do us harm, we have the will not to drink; but although this is an important distinction it is not a fundamental one; what incites us to drink is a passion, what prevents us is another passion, one more general and stronger, the desire not to die, and because this passion by meeting with and fighting another produces in all our being a powerful tension, it is none the less a passion, even if we ought not to say that it is a still more impassioned passion.

Locke's Theory of Politics. — In politics Locke was the adversary of Hobbes, whose theories of absolutism have already been noticed. He did not believe that the natural state was the war of all against all. He believed men formed societies not to escape cannibalism, but more easily to guarantee and protect their natural rights: ownership, personal liberty, legitimate defence. Society only exists to protect these rights, and the reason of its existence lies in this duty to defend them. The sovereign therefore is not the saviour of the nation, he is its law-maker and magistrate. If he violates the rights of man, he acts so directly contrary to his mission and his mandate that insurrection against him is legitimate. The "wise Locke," as Voltaire always called him, was the inventor of the Rights of Man.

In religious politics he was equally liberal and advocated the separation of Church and State; the State, according to him, should not have any religion of its own, its province being only to protect equally the liberty of all denominations.

Locke was discussed minutely by Leibnitz, who, without accepting the innate ideas of Descartes, did not accept the ideas through sensation of Locke, and said: "There is nothing in the intelligence which has not first been in the senses," granted . . . "except the intelligence itself." The intelligence has not innate ideas born ready made; but it possesses forms of its own in which the ideas arrange themselves and take shape, and this is the due province of the intelligence. And it was these forms which later on Kant was to call the categories of the intellect, and at bottom Descartes meant nothing else by his innate ideas. Locke exerted a prodigious and even imperious influence over the French philosophers of the eighteenth century.

CHAPTER IV.

THE ENGLISH PHILOSOPHERS OF THE EIGHTEENTH CENTURY.

Berkeley : Highly Idealist Philosophy which regarded Matter as Non-existent.
David Hume : Sceptical Philosophy.
The Scottish School : Common Sense Philosophy.

BERKELEY.—To the "sensualist" Locke succeeded Berkeley, the unrestrained "idealist," like him an Englishman. He began to write when very young, continued to write until he was sixty, and died at sixty-eight. He neither believed in matter, nor in the external world. There was the whole of his philosophy. Why did he not believe in them ? Because all thinkers are agreed that we cannot know whether we see the external world *as it is*. Then, if we do not know it, why do we affirm that it exists ? We know nothing about it. Now we ought to build up the world only with what we know of it, and to do otherwise is not philosophy but yielding to imagination. What is it that we know of the world ? Our ideas, and nothing but our ideas. Very well then, let us say : there are only ideas. But whence do these ideas come to us ? To explain them as coming from the external world which we have never seen is to explain obscurity by denser darkness. They are spiritual, they come to us without doubt from a spirit, from God. This is possible, it is not illogical, and Berkeley believes it.

This doctrine regarded by the eyes of common sense may appear a mere phantasy; but Berkeley saw in it many things of high importance and great use. If you believe in matter, you can believe in matter only, and that is materialism with its moral consequences, which are immoral; if you believe in matter and in God, you are so hampered by this dualism that you do not know how to separate nature from God, and it therefore comes to pass that you see God in matter, which is called pantheism. In a word, between us and God Berkeley has suppressed matter in order that we should come, as it were, into direct contact with God. He derives much from Malebranche, and it may be said he only pushes his theories to their extreme. Although a bishop, he was not checked, like Descartes, by the idea of God not being able to deceive us, and he answered that God does not deceive us, that He gives us ideas and that it is we who deceive ourselves by attributing them to any other origin than to Him; nor was he checked, like Malebranche, by the authority of Scripture, which in Genesis portrays God creating matter. He only saw there, no doubt, a symbolical sense, a simple way of speaking according to the comprehension of the multitude.

David Hume.—David Hume, a Scotsman, better known, at least in his own times, as the historian of England than as philosopher, nevertheless well merits consideration in the latter category. David Hume believes in nothing, and, in consequence, it may be said that he is not a philosopher; he has no philosophic system. He has no philosophic system, it is true; but he is a critic of philosophy, and therefore he philosophises. Matter has no existence; as we know nothing about it, we should not say it exists. But we ourselves, we exist. All that we can know about that is that in us there is a succession of ideas, of representations; but *we*, but *I*, what is that? Of that we know nothing. We are present at a series of pictures, and we may call their totality the *ego;* but we do not grasp ourselves as a thing of unity, as an individual. We are the spectators of an inward dramatic piece behind which we can see no author. There is no more reason to believe in *oneself* than in the external world.

Innate Ideas.—As for innate ideas, they are simply general ideas, which are general delusions. We believe, for instance, that every effect has a cause, or, to express it more correctly, that everything has a cause. What do we know about it? What do we see? That one thing follows another, succeeds to another. What tells us that the latter proceeds from the former, that the thing B must necessarily come, owing to the thing A existing? We believe it because every time the thing A has been, the thing B has come. Well, let us say that every time A has been (thus far) B has come; and say no more. There are regular successions, but we are completely ignorant whether there are causes for them.

The Liberty and Morality of Hume.—It results from this that for Hume there is no liberty. Very obviously; for when we believe ourselves free, it is because we believe we can fix upon ourselves as a cause. Now the word "cause" means nothing. We are a succession of phenomena very absolutely determined. The proof is that we foresee and nearly always accurately (and we could always foresee accurately if we completely knew the character of the persons and the influences acting on them) what people we know will do, which would be impossible if they did as they wished. And I, at the very moment when I am absolutely sure I am doing such and such a thing because I desired to, I see my friend smile as he says: "I was sure you would do that. See,

I wrote it down on this piece of paper." He understood me as a necessity, when I felt myself to be free. And he, reciprocally, will believe himself free in doing a thing I would have wagered to a certainty that he would not fail to do.

What system of morality can Hume have with these principles? First of all, he protests against those who should deduce from his principles the immorality of his system. (Take care, said he wittily (just like Spinoza, by the way) it is the partisans of free will who are immoral.) No doubt! It is when there is liberty that there is no responsibility. I am not responsible for my actions if they have no connexion in me with anything durable or constant. I have committed murder. Truly it is by chance, if it was by an entirely isolated determination, entirely detached from the rest of my character, and momentary; and I am only infinitesimally responsible. But if all my actions are linked together, are conditional upon one another, dependent on one another, if I have committed murder it is because I am an assassin at every moment of my life or nearly so, and then, oh! how responsible I am!

Note that this is the line taken up by judges, since they make careful investigation of the antecedents of the accused. They find him all the more culpable if he has always shown bad instincts.—Therefore they find him the more responsible, the more he has been compelled by necessity.—Yes.

Hume then does not believe himself "foreclosed" in morality; he does not believe he is forbidden by his principles to have a system of morality and he has one. It is a morality of sentiment. We have in us the instinct of happiness and we seek happiness; but we have also in us an instinct of goodwill which tends to make us seek the general happiness, and reason tells us that there is conciliation or rather concordance between these two instincts, because it is only in the general happiness that we find our particular happiness.

The Scottish School. Reid: Stewart.—The Scottish School (end of the eighteenth century) was pre-eminently a school of men who attached themselves to common sense and were excellent moralists. We must at any rate mention Thomas Reid and Dugald Stewart. They were bent especially on opposing the transcendent idealism of Berkeley and the scepticism of David Hume, also in some measure Locke's doctrine of the blank sheet. They reconstituted the human mind and even the world (which had been so to speak driven off in vapour by their predecessors), much as they were in the time of Descartes. Let us believe (they said) in the reality of the external world, let us believe that there are causes and effects, let us believe there is an *ego*, a human person whom we directly apprehend, and who is a cause; let us believe that we are free and that we are responsible because we are free, etc. They were, pre-eminently, excellent describers of states of the soul, admirable psychological moralists and they were the ancestors of the highly remarkable pleiad of English psychologists of the nineteenth century.

CHAPTER V.

FRENCH PHILOSOPHERS OF THE EIGHTEENTH CENTURY.

Voltaire a Disciple of Locke.
Rousseau a Free-thinking Christian, but deeply imbued with Religious Sentiments.
Diderot a capricious Materialist.
D'Holbach and Helvetius avowed Materialists.
Condillac a Philosopher of Sensations.

VOLTAIRE: ROUSSEAU.—The French philosophy of the eighteenth century, fairly feeble it must be avowed, seemed as if dominated by the English philosophy, excepting Berkeley, but especially by Locke and David Hume, more particularly Locke, who was the intellectual deity of those Frenchmen of that epoch who were interested in philosophy.

Whenever Voltaire dealt with philosophy, he was only the echo of Locke whose depths he failed to fathom, and to whom he has done some injury, for reading Locke only through Voltaire has led to the belief that Locke was superficial.

Rousseau was both the disciple and adversary of Hobbes, as often occurs, and dealt out to the public the doctrines of Hobbes in an inverted form, making the state of nature angelic instead of infernal, and putting the government of all by all in the place of government by one, invariably reaching the same point with a simple difference of form; for if Hobbes argued for despotism exercised by one over all, Rousseau argued for the despotism of all over each. In *Emile*, he was incontestably inspired by the ideas of Locke on education in some degree, but in my opinion less than has been asserted. On nearly all sides it has been asserted that Rousseau exercised great influence over Kant. I know that Kant felt infinite admiration for Rousseau, but of the influence of Rousseau upon Kant I have never been able to discover a trace.

Diderot: Helvetius: D'Holbach.—It was particularly on David Hume that Diderot depended. The difference, which is great, is that David Hume in his scepticism remained a grave, reserved man, well-bred and discreet, and was only a sceptic, whilst Diderot was violent in denial and a man of paradoxes and jests, both impertinent and cynical.

It is almost ridiculous in a summary history of philosophy to name as sub-Diderots, if one may so express it, Helvetius and D'Holbach, who were merely wits believing themselves philosophers, and who were not always wits.

Condillac.—Condillac belongs to another category. He was a very serious philosopher and a vigorous thinker. An exaggerated disciple of

Locke, while the latter admitted sensation *and* reflection as the origin of ideas, Condillac only admitted pure sensation and transformed sensation, that is to say, sensation transforming itself. The definition of man that he deduces from these principles is very celebrated and it is interesting: "The *ego* of each man is only the collection of the sensations that he feels and of those his memory recalls; it is the consciousness of what he is combined with the recollection of what he has been." To Condillac, the idea is a sensation which has fixed itself and which has been renewed and vivified by others; desire is a sensation which wishes to be repeated and seeks what opportunity offers for its renewal, and the will itself is only the most potent of desires. Condillac was voluntarily and systematically limited, but his system is well knit and presented in admirably clear and precise language.

CHAPTER VI.

KANT.

Kant reconstructed all Philosophy by supporting it on Morality.

KNOWLEDGE.—Kant, born at Königsberg in 1724, was professor there all his life and died there in 1804. Nothing happened to him except the possession of genius. He had commenced with the theological philosophy in use in his country, that of Wolf, which on broad lines was that of Leibnitz. But he early read David Hume, and the train of thought of the sceptical Englishman at least gave him the idea of submitting all philosophic ideas to a severe and close criticism.

He first of all asked himself what the true value is of our knowledge and what knowledge is. We believe generally that it is the things which give us the knowledge that we have of them. But, rather, is it not we who impose on things the forms of our mind and is not the knowledge that we believe we have of things only the knowledge which we take of the laws of our mind by applying it to things? This is what is most probable. We perceive the things by moulds, so to speak, which are in ourselves and which give them their shapes and they would be shapeless and chaotic were it otherwise. Consequently, it is necessary to distinguish the matter and the form of our knowledge: the matter of the knowledge is the things themselves. The form of our knowledge is ourselves: "Our experimental knowledge is a compound of what we receive from impressions and of what our individual faculty of knowing draws from itself on the occasion of these impressions."

SENSIBILITY: UNDERSTANDING: REASON.—Those who believe that all we think proceeds from the senses are therefore wrong; so too are those wrong who believe that all we think proceeds from ourselves. To say, Matter is an appearance, and to say, Ideas are appearances, are equally false doctrines. Now we know by sensibility, by understanding, and by reason. By sensibility we receive the impression of phenomena; by the understanding we impose on these impressions their forms, and link them up together; by reason we give ourselves general ideas of things—universal ones, going beyond or believing they go beyond the data, even when linked up and systematised.

Let us analyse sensibility, understanding, and reason. Sensibility already has the forms it imposes on things. These forms are time and space. Time and space are not given us by matter like colour, smell, taste or sound; they are not perceived by the senses ; they are therefore the forms of our sensibility : we can only feel according to time and space, by lodging what we feel in space and time ; these are the conditions of sensibility. Phenomena are thus perceived by us under the laws of space and of time. What do they become in us ? They are seized by the understanding, which also has its forms, its powers of classification, of arrangement, and of connexion. Its forms or powers, or, putting it more exactly, its active forms are, for example, the conception of quantity being always equal : through all phenomena the quantity of substance remains always the same ; the conception of causality : everything has a cause and every cause has an effect and it is ever thus. Those are the conditions of our understanding, those without which we do not understand and the forms which within us we impose on all things in order to understand them.

It is thus that we know the world ; which is tantamount to stating that the world only exists, so far as we are concerned, so long as we think so. Reason would go further : it would seize the most general, the universal, beyond experience, beyond the limited and restricted systematizations established by the understanding ; to know, for instance, the first cause of all causes, the last and collective end, so to speak, of all purposes; to know "why is there something"? and "in view of what end is there something"? in fact, to answer all the questions of infinity and eternity. Be sure that it cannot. How could it? It only operates, can only operate, on the data of experience and the systematisations of the understanding, which classify experience but do not go beyond it. Only operating upon that, having nothing except that as matter, how could it itself go beyond experience? It cannot. It is only (a highly important fact, and one which must on no account be forgotten)—it is only a sign, merely a witness. It is the sign that the human spirit has need of the absolute; it is itself that need; without that it would not exist; it is the witness of our invincible insistence on knowing and of our tendency to estimate that we know nothing if we only know something; it is itself that insistence and that tendency: without that it would not exist. Let us pause there for the moment. Man only knows of nature those impressions which he receives from it, co-ordinated by the forms of sensibility, and further the ideas of it which he preserves co-ordinated by the forms of his understanding. This is very little. It is all, if we only consider pure reason.

PRACTICAL REASON.—*But* there is perhaps

another reason, or another aspect of reason—to wit, practical reason. What is practical reason? Something in us tells us: you should act, and you should act in such a way; you should act rightly; this is not right, so do not do it; that is right, do it. As a fact this is uncontestable. What is the explanation? From what data of experience, from what systematisation of the understanding has our mind borrowed this? Where has it got it? Does nature yield obedience to a "you ought"? Not at all. It exists, and it develops and it goes its way, according to our way of seeing it in time and space, and that is all. Does the understanding furnish the idea of "you ought?" By no means; it gives us ideas of quantity, of quality, of cause and effect, etc., and that is all; there is no "you ought" in all that. Therefore this "you ought" is purely human; it is the only principle which comes exactly from ourselves only. It might therefore well be the very foundation of us.—It may be an illusion.—No doubt, but it is highly remarkable that *it exists*, though nothing gives it birth or is of a nature to give it birth. An illusion is a weakness of the senses or an error of logic and is thus explained; but an illusion in itself and by itself and only proceeding from itself is most singular and not to be explained as an illusion. Hence it remains that it is a reality, a reality of our nature, and given the coercive force of its voice and act, it is the most real reality there is in us.

THE CATEGORICAL IMPERATIVE.—Thus, at least, thought Kant, and he said: There is a practical reason which does not go beyond experience and does not seek to go beyond it; but which does not depend on it, is absolutely separated from it, and is its own (human) experience by itself. This practical reason says to us: you ought to do good. The crowd call it conscience; I call it in a general way practical reason, and I call it the categorical imperative when I take it in its principle, without taking into account the applications which I foresee. Why this name? To distinguish it clearly; for we feel ourselves commanded by other things than it, but not in the same way. We feel ourselves commanded by prudence, for instance, which tells us: do not run down that staircase *if* you do not wish to break your neck; we feel ourselves commanded by the conventions which say: be polite *if* you do not wish men to leave you severely alone, etc. But conscience does not say *if* to us: it says bluntly "you ought" without consideration of what may or may not happen, and it is even part of its character to scorn all consideration of consequences. It would tell us: run down that staircase to save that child even at the risk of breaking your neck. Because of that I call all the other commandments made to us hypothetical imperatives and that of conscience, alone, the categorical or absolute imperative. Here is a definite result.

MORALITY, THE LAW OF MAN.—Yet reflect: if the foregoing be true, morality is the very law of man, his especial law as the law of the tree is to spread in roots and branches. Well. But for man to be able to obey his law he must be free, must be able to do what he wishes. That is certain. Then it must be believed that we are free, for were we not, we could not obey our law; and the moral law would be absurd. The moral law is the *sign* that we are free. Compared to this, all the other proofs of freedom are worthless or weak. We are free because we must be so in order to do the good which our law commands us to do.

Let us examine further. I do what is right in order to obey the law; but, when I have done it, I have the idea that it would be unjust that I should be punished for it, or that I should not be rewarded for it, that it would be unjust were there not concordance between right and happiness. As it happens, virtue is seldom rewarded in this world and often is even punished; it draws misfortune or evil on him who practises it.

Would not that be the sign that there are two worlds of which we only see one? Would not that be the sign that virtue unrewarded here will be rewarded elsewhere *in order that there should not be injustice?* It is highly probable that this is so.

But for that it is necessary that the soul be immortal. It is so, since it is necessary that it should be. The moral law is accomplished and consummated in rewards or penalties beyond the grave, which pre-suppose the immortality of the soul. All the other proofs of the immortality of the soul are worthless or feeble beside this one which demonstrates that were there no immortality of the soul there would be no morality.

God.—And, finally, if justice is one day to be done, this supposes a Judge. It is neither ourselves who in another life will do justice to ourselves nor yet some force of circumstances which will do it to us. It is necessary to have an intelligence conceiving justice and a will to realise it. God is this intelligence and this will.

All the other proofs of God are weak or worthless beside this one. The existence of God has been deduced from the idea of God: if we have the idea of God, it is necessary that He should exist. A weak proof, for we can have an idea which does not correspond with an object. The existence of God has been deduced from the idea of causality; for all that is, a cause is necessary, this cause is God. A weak proof; for things being as they are, there is necessity for . . . cause; but *a* cause and a *single* cause, why? There could be a series of causes to infinity and thus the cause of the world could be the world itself. The existence of God has been deduced from the idea of *design* well carried out. The composition, the ordering of this world is admired; this world is well made; it is like a clock. The clock supposes a clock-maker; the fine composition of the world supposes an intelligence which conceived a work to be made and which made it. Perhaps; but this consideration only leads to the idea of a manipulation of matter, of a demiurge, as the Greeks said, of an architect, but not to the idea of a *Creator;* it may even lead only to the idea of several architects and the Greeks perfectly possessed the idea of a fine artistic order existing in the world when they believed in a great number of deities. This proof also is therefore weak, although Kant always treats it with respect.

The sole convincing proof is the existence of the moral law in the heart of man. For the moral law to be accomplished, for it not to be merely a tyrant over man, for it to be realized in all its fulness, weighing on man here but rewarding him infinitely elsewhere, which means there is justice in all that, it is necessary that somewhere there should be an absolute realizer of justice. God must exist for the world to be moral.

Why is it necessary for the world to be moral? Because an immoral world with even a single moral being in it would be a very strange thing.

Thus, whilst the majority of philosophers deduced human liberty from God, and the spirituality of the soul from human liberty, the immortality of the soul from human spirituality and morality from human immortality, Kant starts from morality as from the incontestable fact, and from morality deduces liberty, and from liberty spirituality, and God from the immortality of the soul with the consequent realization of justice.

He has effected an extraordinarily powerful reversal of the argument generally employed.

The Influence of Kant.—The influence of Kant has been incomparable or, if you will, comparable only to those of Plato, Zeno and Epicurus. Half at least of the European philosophy of the nineteenth century has proceeded from him and is closely connected with him. Even in our own day, pragmatism, as it is called—that is, the doctrine which lays down that morality is the measure of truth and that an idea is only true if it be morally useful—is perhaps an alteration of Kantism, a Kantian heresy, but entirely penetrated with and, as it were, excited by the spirit of Kant.

CHAPTER VII.

THE NINETEENTH CENTURY.—GERMANY.

The great Reconstructors of the World, analogous to the first Philosophers of Antiquity.
Great General Systems, Fichte, Schelling, Hegel, etc.

FICHTE. — Fichte, embarrassed by what remained of experience in the ideas of Kant, by the part, restricted though it was, which Kant left to things in the external world, completely suppressed the external world, like Berkeley, and affirmed the existence of the human *ego* alone. Kant said that the world furnished us with the matter of the idea and that we furnished the form. According to Fichte form and matter alike came from us. What then is sensation? It is nothing except the pause of the *ego* encountering what is not self, the impact of the *ego* against what limits it.—But then the external world does exist, for how could our mind be encountered by nothing and there be an impact of our mind against nothing?—But this non-self that encounters self is precisely a product of self, a product of the imagination which creates an object, which projects outside us an appearance before which we pause as before something real which should be outside us.

This theory is very difficult to understand, but indicates a very fine effort of the mind.

Yet outside ourselves is there anything ?—There is pure spirit, God. What is God ? For Fichte He is moral order (a very evident recollection of Kant). Morality is God and God is morality. We are in God, and it is the whole of religion, when we do our duty without any regard to the consequences of our actions; we are outside God, and it is atheism, when we act in view of what results our actions may have. And thus morality and religion run into one another, and religion is only morality in its plenitude and complete morality is the whole of religion. "The holy, the beautiful, and the good are the immediate apparition [if it could be] in us of the essence of God."

Schelling.—Schelling desired to correct what, according to him, was too radical in the idealism of Fichte. He restored the external world; for him the *non-ego* and the *ego* both exist and the two are *nature*, nature which is the object in the world regarded by man, the subject when it regards man, subject and object according to the case; in itself and in its totality neither subject nor object, but absolute, unlimited, indeterminate. Confronting this world (that is nature and man) there is another world which is God. God is the infinite and the perfect, and particularly the perfect and infinite will. The world that we know is a debasement from that without our being able to conceive how the perfect can be degraded, and how an emanation of the perfect can be imperfect and how the non-being can come out of being, since relatively to the infinite, the finite has no existence and relatively to perfection, the imperfect is nothing.

It appears however that it is thus, and that the world is an emanation of God in which He degrades Himself and a degradation of God such that it opposes itself to Him as nothing to everything. It is a fall. The fall of man in the Scriptures may give an idea, however distant, of that.

HEGEL.—Hegel, a contemporary of Schelling, and often in contradiction to him, is the philosopher of "*becoming*" and of the idea which always "becomes" something. The essence of all is the idea, but the idea in progress; the idea makes itself a thing according to a rational law which is inherent in it, and the thing makes itself an idea in the sense that the idea contemplating the thing it has become thinks it and fills itself with it in order to become yet another thing, always following the rational law; and this very evolution, all this evolution, all this becoming, is that absolute for which we are always searching behind things, at the root of things and which is *in* the things themselves.

The rationally active is everything; and activity and reality are synonyms and all reality is active and what is not active is not real, and what is not active has no existence.

Let not this activity be regarded as always advancing forward; the becoming is not a river which flows; activity is activity and retro-activity. The cause is cause of the effect, but also the effect is cause of its cause. In fact the cause would not be cause if it had no effect; it is therefore thanks to its effect, because of its effect, that the cause is cause; and therefore the effect is the cause of the cause as much as the cause is cause of the effect.

A government is the effect of the character of a people, and the character of a people is the effect also of its government; my son proceeds from me, but he reacts on me and because I am his father I have the character which I gave him, more pronounced than before, etc.

Hence, all effect is cause as all cause is effect, which everybody has recognised, but in addition all effect is cause of its cause and in consequence to speak in common language all effect is cause forward and backward and the line of causes and effects is not a straight line but a circle

THE DEISM OF HEGEL.—God disappears from all that. No, Hegel is very formally a deist; but he sees God in the total of things and not outside things, yet distinct. In what way distinct? In this, that God is the totality of things considered not in themselves but in the spirit that animates them and the force that urges them, and because the soul is of necessity in the body, united to the body, that is no reason why it should not be distinct from it. And having taken up this position, Hegel is a deist and even accepts proofs of the existence of God which are regarded by some as hackneyed. He accepts them, only holding them not exactly as proofs, but as reasons for belief, and as highly faithful descriptions of the necessary elevation of the soul to God. For example, the ancient philosophers proved the existence of God by the contemplation of the marvels of the universe: "That is not a 'proof,'" said Hegel, "that is not a proof, but it is a great reason for belief; for it is an exposition, a very exact although incomplete account rendered of the fact that by contemplation of the world the human mind rises to God." Now this fact is of singular importance: it indicates that it is impossible to think strongly without thinking of God. "When the passage [although insufficiently logical] from the finite to the infinite does not take place, it may be said that there is no thought." Now this is a reason for belief.

After the same fashion, the philosophers have said "from the moment that we imagine God, the reason is that He is." Kant ridicules this proof. Granted, it is not an invincible proof, but this fact alone that we cannot imagine God without affirming His existence indicates a tendency of our mind which is to relate finite thought to infinite thought and not to admit an imperfect thought which should not have its source in a perfect thought; and that is rather an invincible belief than a proof, but that this belief is invincible and necessary in itself is an extremely commanding proof, although a relative one.

His Political Philosophy.—The philosophy of the human mind and political philosophy according to Hegel are these. Primitive man is mind, reason, conscience, but he is so only potentially, as the philosophers express it, that is to say, he is so only in that he is capable of becoming so. Really, practically, he is only instincts: he is egoist, like the animals [it should be said like the greater part of the animals] and follows his egoistical appetites. Society, in whatever manner it has managed to constitute itself, transforms him and his "becoming" commences. From the sexual instinct it makes marriage, from capture it forms regulated proprietorship, out of defence against violence it makes legal punishment, etc. Henceforth, and all his evolution tends to that, man proceeds to substitute in himself the general will for the particular will; he tends to dis-individualise himself. The general will, founded upon general utility, is that the man be married, father, head of a family, good husband, good father, good relative, good citizen. All that man ought to be in consideration of the general will which he has put in the place of his own, and which he has made his own will. That is the first advance.

It is realized (always imperfectly) in the smallest societies, in the cities, in the little Greek republics, for example.

Here is the second advance. By war, by conquest, by annexations, by more gentle means when possible, the stronger cities subdue the weaker, and the great State is created. The great State has a more important part than the city; it continues to substitute the general will for the particular wills; but, *in addition*, it is an idea, a great civilizing idea, benevolent, *elevating*, aggrandizing, to which private interests must and should be sacrificed. Such were the Romans who considered themselves, not without reason, as the legislators and civilizers of the world.

The Ideal Form of State.—Putting aside for a while the continuation of this subject, what political form should the great State take to conform to its destiny? Assuredly the monarchical form; for the republican form is always too individualist. To Hegel, the Greeks and even the Romans seem to have conceded too much to individual liberty or to the interests of class, of caste; they possessed an imperfect idea of the rights and functions of the State. The ideal form of the State is monarchy. It is necessary for the State to be contracted, gathered up and personified in a prince who can be personally loved, who can be reverenced, which is precisely what is needed. These great States are only really great if they possess strong cohesion; it is therefore necessary that they should be nationalities, as it is called, that is that they should be inwardly very united and highly homogeneous by community of race, religion, customs, language, etc. The idea to be realized by a State can only be accomplished if there be a sufficient community of ideas in the people constituting it. However the great State will be able to and even ought to conquer and annex the small ones in order to become stronger and more capable, being stronger, of realizing its idea. Only this should be done merely when it is certain or clearly apparent that it represents an id… as against a people which does not, or that … presents a better, greater and nobler idea tha… that represented by the people it attacks.

WAR.—But, as each people will always find its own idea finer than that of another, how is this to be recognized ?—By victory itself. It is victory which proves that a people . . . Was stronger than another ! — Not only stronger materially but representing a greater, more practical, more fruitful idea than the other ; for it is precisely the idea which supports a people and renders it strong. Thus, victory is the sign of the moral superiority of a people, and in consequence force indicates where right is and is indistinguishable from right itself, and we must not say as may have already perhaps been said : "might excels right," but "might is right" or "right is might."

For example [Hegel might have said] France was "apparently" within her rights in endeavouring to conquer Europe from 1792 to 1815 ; for she represented an idea, the revolutionary idea, which she might consider, and which many besides the French did consider, an advance and a civilizing idea ; but she was beaten, *which proves* that the idea was false ; and before this demonstration by events is it not true that the republican or Cæsarian idea is inferior to that of traditional monarchy? Hegel would certainly have reasoned thus on this point.

Therefore war is eternal and must be so. It is history itself, being the condition of history; it is even the evolution of humanity, being the condition of that evolution; therefore, it is divine. Only it is purifying itself; formerly men only fought, or practically always, from ambition; now wars are waged for principles, to effect the triumph of an idea which has a future, and which contains the future, over one that is out of date and decayed. The future will see a succession of the triumphs of might which, by definition, will be triumphs of right and which will be triumphs of increasingly fine ideas over ideas that are barbarous and justly condemned to perish.

Hegel has exercised great influence on the ideas of the German people both in internal and external politics.

ART, SCIENCE AND RELIGION.—The ideas of Hegel on art, science and religion are the following: Under the shelter of the State which is necessary for their peaceful development in security and liberty, science, literature, art and religion pursue aims not superior to but other than those of the State. They seek, without detaching the individual from the society, to unite him to the whole world. Science makes him know all it can of nature and its laws; literature, by studying man in himself and in his relations with the world, imbues him with the sentiment of the possible concordance of the individual with the universe; the arts make him love creation by unravelling and bringing into the light and into relief all that is beautiful in it relatively to man, and, all that in consequence should render it lovely, respected, and dear to him; religion, finally, seeks to be a bond between all men and a bond between all men and God; it sketches the plan of universal brotherhood which is ideally the last state of humanity, a state which no doubt it will never attain, but which it is essential it should imagine and believe to be possible, without which it always would be drawn towards animality more and much more than it is.

The Hegelian philosophy has exercised an immense influence throughout Europe not only on philosophic studies, but on history, art, and literature. It may be regarded as the last "universal system" and as the most daring that has been attempted by the human mind.

Schopenhauer.—Schopenhauer was the philosopher of the will. Persuaded, like Leibnitz, that man is an epitome and a picture of the world and that the world resembles us (which is hypothetical) he takes up the thought of Leibnitz, changing and transforming it thus: All the universe is not thought, but all the universe is will; thought is only an accident of the will which appears in the superior animals; but the will, which is the foundation of man, is the foundation of all; the universe is a compound of wills that act. All beings are wills which possess organs conformed to their purpose. It is *the will to be* which gave claws to the lion, tusks to the boar and intelligence to man, because he was the most unarmed of animals, just as to one who becomes blind it gives extraordinarily sensitive and powerful sense of hearing, smell, and touch. Plants strive towards light by their tops and towards moisture by their roots; the seed turns itself in the earth to send forth its stalk upwards and its rootlet downward. In minerals there are "constant tendencies" which are nothing but obscure wills; what we currently term weight, fluidity, impenetrability, electricity, chemical affinities, are nothing but natural wills or inconscient wills. Because of this, the diverse wills opposing and clashing with one another, the world is a war of all against all and of *everything* literally against *everything;* and the world is a scene of carnage.

The truth is that will is an evil and is the evil. What is needed for happiness is to kill the will, to destroy the wish to be.—But this would be the end of existence ?—And in fact to be no more or not to be at all is the true happiness and it would be necessary to blow up the whole world in an explosion for it to escape unhappiness. At least, as Buddhism desired and, in some degree, though less, Christianity also, it is necessary to make an approach to death by a kind of reduction to the absolute minimum of will, by detachment and renunciation pushed as far as can be.

NIETZSCHE.—A very respectful but highly independent and untractable pupil of Schopenhauer, Nietzsche " turns Schopenhauer inside out " as it were, saying : Yes, assuredly the will to be is everything ; but precisely because of that it is essential not to oppose but to follow it and to follow it as far as it will lead us. But is it not true that it will lead to suffering ? Be sure of that, but in suffering there is an intoxication of pain which is quite comprehensible ; for it is the intoxication of the will in action ; and this intoxication is an enjoyment too and in any case a good thing ; for it is the end to which we are urged by our nature composed of will and of hunger for existence. Now wisdom, like happiness, is to follow our nature. The happiness and wisdom of man is to obey his will for power, as the wisdom and happiness of water is to flow towards the sea.

From these ideas is derived a morality of violence which can be legitimately regarded as immoral and which, in any case, is neither Buddhist nor Christian, but which is susceptible of several interpretations, all the more so because Nietzsche, who was a poet, never fails, whilst always artististically very fine, to fall into plenty of contradictions.

CHAPTER VIII.

THE NINETEENTH CENTURY—ENGLAND.

The Doctrines of Evolution and of Transformism: Lamarck (French), Darwin, Spencer.

TRANSFORMISM AND EVOLUTION.—The great philosophic invention of the English of the nineteenth century has been the idea, based on a wide knowledge of natural history, that there never was creation. The animal species had been considered by all the philosophers (except Epicurus and the Epicureans) as being created once and for all and remaining invariable. Nothing of the kind. Matter, eternally fruitful, has transformed itself first into plants, then into lower animals, then into higher animals, then into man; our ancestor is the fish; tracing back yet more remotely our ancestor is the plant. Transformation (hence the name *transformism*), discrimination and separation of species, the strongest individuals of each kind alone surviving and creating descendants in their image which constitute a species; evolution (hence the name *evolutionism*) of living nature thus operating from the lowest types to the highest and therefore the most complicated; there is nothing but that in the world.

Lamarck, Darwin, Spencer.—The Frenchman Lamarck in the eighteenth century had already conceived this idea; Darwin, purely a naturalist, set it forth clearly, Spencer again stated it and drew from it consequences of general philosophy. Thus, to Spencer, the evolutionist theory contains no immorality. On the contrary, the progressive transformation of the human species is an ascent towards morality; from egoism is born altruism because the species, seeking its best law and its best condition of happiness, perceives a greater happiness in altruism; seeking its best law and its best condition of happiness, perceives that a greater happiness lies in order, regular life, social life, etc.; so that humanity raises itself to a higher and yet higher morality by the mere fact of adapting itself better to the conditions of the life of humanity. Morality develops physiologically as the germ becomes the stem and the bud becomes the flower.

As for religion it is the domain of the unknowable. That is not to assert that it is nothing. On the contrary it is something formidable and immense. It is the feeling that something, apart from all that we know, surpasses us and that we shall never know it. Now this feeling at the same time maintains us in a humility highly favourable to the health of the soul and also in a serene confidence in the mysterious being who presides over universal evolution and who, no doubt, is the all-powerful and eternal soul of it.

CHAPTER IX.

THE NINETEENTH CENTURY—FRANCE.

**The Eclectic School: Victor Cousin.
The Positivist School: Auguste Comte.
The Kantist School: Renouvier.
Independent and complex Positivists: Taine, Renan.**

LAROMIGUIÈRE: ROYER-COLLARD. — Emerging from the school of Condillac, France saw Laromiguière who was a sort of softened Condillac, less trenchant, and not insensible to the influence of Rousseau; but he was little more than a clear and elegant professor of philosophy. Royer-Collard introduced into France the Scottish philosophy (Thomas Reid, Dugald Stewart) and did not depart from it or go beyond it; but he set it forth with magnificent authority and with a remarkable invention of clear and magisterial formulæ.

MAINE DE BIRAN.—Maine de Biran was a renovator. He attached himself to Descartes linking the chain anew that had for so long been interrupted. He devoted his attention to the notion of *ego*. In full reaction from the "sensualism" of Condillac, he restored a due activity to the *ego*; he made it a force not restricted to the reception of sensations, which transform themselves, but one which seized upon, elaborated, linked together and combined them. For him then, as for Descartes, but from a fresh point of view, the voluntary deed is the primitive deed of the soul and the will is the foundation of man. Also, the will is not all man; man has, so to say, three lives superimposed but very closely inter-united and which cannot do without one another; the life of sensation, the life of will, and the life of love. The life of sensation is almost passive, with a commencement of activity which consists in classifying and organizing the sensations; the life of will is properly speaking the "human" life; the life of love is the life of activity and yet again of will, but which unites the human with the divine life. By the ingenious and profound subtlety of his analyses, Maine de Biran has placed himself in the front rank of French thinkers and, in any case, he is one of the most original.

Victor Cousin and His Disciples.—Victor Cousin, who appears to have been influenced almost concurrently by Maine de Biran, Royer-Collard and the German philosophy, yielded rapidly to a tendency which is characteristically French and is also, perhaps, good, and which consists in seeing "some good in all the opinions," and he was eclectic, that is, a borrower. His maxim, which he had no doubt read in Leibnitz, was that the systems are "true in what they affirm and false in what they deny." Starting thence, he rested upon both the English and German philosophy, correcting one by the other. Personally his tendency was to make metaphysics come from philosophy and to prove God by the human soul and the relations of God with the world by the relations of man with matter. To him God is always an augmented human soul. All philosophies, not to mention all religions, have rather an inclination to consider things thus; but this tendency is particularly marked in Cousin. In the course of his career, which was diversified, for he was at one time a professor and at another a statesman, he varied somewhat, because before 1830 he became very Hegelian, and after 1830 he harked back towards Descartes, endeavouring especially to make philosophic instruction a moral priesthood; highly cautious, very well-balanced, feeling great distrust of the unassailable temerities of the one and in sympathetic relations with the other. What has remained of this eclecticism is an excellent thing, the great regard for the *history* of philosophy, which had never been held in honour in France and which, since Cousin, has never ceased to be so.

The principal disciples of Cousin were Jouffroy,

Damiron, Emile Saisset, and the great moralist Jules Simon, well-known because of the important political part he played.

LAMENNAIS.—Lamennais, long celebrated for his great book: *Essay on Indifference in the Matter of Religion*, then, when he had severed himself from Rome, by his *Words of a Believer* and other works of revolutionary spirit, was above all a publicist; but he was a philosopher, properly speaking, in his *Sketch of a Philosophy*. To him, God is neither the Creator, as understood by the early Christians, nor the Being from whom the world emanates, as others have thought. He has not created the world *from nothing*; but He has created it; He created it from Himself, He made it issue from His substance; and He made it issue by a purely voluntary act. He created it in His own image; it is not man alone who is in the image of God, but the whole world. The three Persons of God, that is the three characteristics, power, intelligence, and love are found —diminished and disfigured indeed, but yet are to be found—in every being in the universe. They are especially our own three powers, under the form of will, reason, sympathy; they are also the three powers of society, under the forms of executive power, deliberation and fraternity. Every being, individual or collective, has in it a principle of death if it cannot reproduce however imperfectly all the three terms of this trinity without the loss of one.

AUGUSTE COMTE.—Auguste Comte, a mathematician, versed also in all sciences, constructed a pre-eminently negative philosophy in spite of his great pretension to replace the negations of the eighteenth century by a positive doctrine; above all else he denied all authority and denied to metaphysics the right of existence. Metaphysics ought not to exist, do not exist, are a mere nothing. We know nothing, we can know nothing, about the commencement or the end of things, or yet their essence or their object; philosophy has always laid down as its task a general explanation of the universe; it is precisely this general explanation, all general explanation of the aggregate of things, which is impossible. This is the negative part of "positivism." It is the only one which has endured and which is the *credo* or rather the *non credo* of a fairly large number of minds.

The affirmative part of the ideas of Comte was this: what can be done is to make a classification of sciences and a philosophy of history. The classification of sciences according to Comte, proceeding from the most simple to the most complex, that is, from mathematics to astronomy, physics, chemistry, biology to end at sociology, is generally considered by the learned as interesting but arbitrary. The philosophy of history, according to Comte, is this: humanity passes through three states: theological, metaphysical, positive. The theological state (antiquity) consists in man explaining everything by continual miracles; the metaphysical state (modern times) consists in man explaining everything by ideas, which he still continues to consider somewhat as beings, by abstractions, entities, vital principle, attraction, gravitation, soul, faculty of the soul, etc. The positive state consists in that man explains and will explain all things, or rather limits himself and will limit himself to verifying them, by the links that he will see they have with one another, links he will content himself with observing and subsequently with controlling by experiment. Also there is always something of the succeeding state in the preceding state and the ancients did not ignore observation, and there is always something of the preceding state in the succeeding state and we have still theological and metaphysical habits of mind, theological and metaphysical "residues," and perhaps it will be always thus; but for theology to decline before metaphysics and metaphysics before science is progress.

Over and above this, Comte in the last portion of his life—as if to prove his doctrine of residues and to furnish an example—founded a sort of religion, a pseudo-religion, the religion of humanity. Humanity must be worshipped in its slow ascent towards intellectual and moral perfection (and, in consequence, we should specially worship humanity to come; but Comte might reply that humanity past and present is venerable because it bears in its womb the humanity of the future). The worship of this new religion is the commemoration and veneration of the dead. These last conceptions, fruits of the sensibility and of the imagination of Auguste Comte, have no relation with the basis of his doctrine.

Renouvier.—After him, by a vigorous reaction, Renouvier restored the philosophy of Kant, depriving it of its too symmetrical, too minutely systematic, too scholastic character and bringing it nearer to facts; from him was to come the doctrine already mentioned, "pragmatism," which measures the truth of every idea by the moral consequence that it contains.

Taine.—Very different and attaching himself to the general ideas of Comte, Hippolyte Taine only believed in what has been observed, experimented and demonstrated; but being also as familiar with Hegel as with Comte, with Spencer as with Condillac, he never doubted that the need of going beyond and escaping from oneself was also a fact, a man fact eternal among humanity and of th fact he took account as of a fact observed and proved, saying if man is on one side a " fierce and lascivious gorilla," on the other side he is a mystic animal and that in "a double nature, mysterious hymen," as Hugo wrote, lay the explanation of all the baseness in ideas and actions as well as all the sublimity in ideas and actions of humanity. Personally he was a Stoic and his practice was the continuous development of the intelligence regarded as the condition and guarantee of morality.

RENAN.—Renan, destined for the ecclesiastical profession and always preserving profound traces of his clerical education, was nevertheless a Positivist and only believed in science, hoping everything from it in youth and continuing to venerate it at least during his mature years. Thus formed, a " Christian Positivist," as has been said, as well as a poet above all else, he could not proscribe metaphysics and had a weakness for them with which perhaps he reproached himself. He extricated himself from this difficulty by declaring all metaphysical conceptions to be only " dreams," but sheltered, so to say, by this concession he had made and this precaution he had taken, he threw himself into the dream with all his heart and reconstituted God, the immortal soul, the future existence, eternity and creation, giving them new, unforeseen and fascinating names. It was only the idea of Providence, that is of the particular and circumstantial intervention of God in human affairs which was intolerable to him and against which he always protested, quoting the phrase of Malebranche "God does not act by particular wills." And yet he paid a compliment, which seems sincere, to the idea of grace, and if there be a particular and circumstantial intervention by God in human affairs, it is certainly grace according to all appearances.

He was above all an amateur of ideas, a dilettante in ideas, toying with them with infinite pleasure, like a superior Greek sophist, and in all French philosophy no one calls Plato to mind more than he does.

He possessed a charming mind, a very lofty character, and was a marvellous writer.

TO-DAY.—The living French philosophers whom we shall content ourselves with naming because they are living and receive contemporary criticism rather than that of history, are MM. Fouillee, Théodule Ribot, Liard, Durckheim, Izoulet, and Bergson.

THE FUTURE OF PHILOSOPHY.—It is impossible to forecast in what direction philosophy will move. The summary history we have been able to trace sufficiently shows, as it seems to us, that it has no regular advance such that by seeing how it has progressed one can conjecture what path it will pursue. It seems in no sense to depend, or at all events, to depend remarkably little, at any period, on the general state of civilization around it, and even for those who believe in a philosophy of history there is not, as it appears to me, a philosophy of the history of philosophy. The only thing that can be affirmed is that philosophy will always exist in response to a need of the human mind, and that it will always be both an effort to gather scientific discoveries into some great general ideas and an effort to go beyond science and to seek as it can the meaning of the universal enigma; so that neither philosophy properly speaking, nor even metaphysics will ever disappear. Nietzsche has said that life is only valuable as the instrument of knowledge. However eager humanity may be and become for branches of knowledge, it will be always passionately and indefatigably anxious about complete knowledge.

THE END.

INDEX OF NAMES CITED.

Abelard - - - 74-77
Ænesidemus - - 46
Agrippa - - - 46
Agrippa (Cornelius) - 91
Ailly (Pierre d') - - 88
Albertus Magnus - - 78
Alexander the Great 26, 31, 32, 44
Anaxagoras - - 5, 11, 20
Anaximander - - 4
Anselm (St.) - 70-73, 110
Antisthenes - - - 31, 35
Apollodorus - - 38
Arcesilaus - - - 45
Arete - - - - 33
Aristippus - 32, 35, 36, 38, 103
Aristobulus - - - 59
Aristo - - - - 42
Aristophanes - - - 14
Aristotle 26-29, 30, 44, 79, 80, 86, 92, 93
Arius - - - - 56
Arnauld - - - 126
Atticus - - - 39
Augustine (St.) - 61-64, 68, 71
Averroes - - - 70
Avicenna - - 70

Bacon (Francis) - 97-100, 125
Bacon (Roger) - - 85, 97
Beaconsfield - - - 37
Bergson - - - 194
Berkeley - 146-148, 152, 168
Bonaventura (St.) - - 84
Bossuet - - - 126
Bruno (Giordano) - - 95
Brutus - - 42
Buridan - - 88

Calvin - - - - 57, 94
Campanella - - - 95-97
Cardan - - - - 91
Carneades - - - 46
Cato - - - - 42
Champeaux (William of) 74, 75
Charles the Bald - - 68
Christina of Sweden - 107
Chrysippus - - - 42
Cicero - - 41, 42, 46
Cleanthes - - - 42
Clement (St.) of Alexandria 60
Comte (Auguste) - 97, 189-191
Condillac - 155-156, 185, 191
Corneille - - - 114
Cousin (Victor) 126, 186, 187
Crantor - - - 30
Crates - - 30, 32, 40

Damiron - - - 187
Darwin - - - 183
Democritus - - - 8, 9
Descartes 95, 107-131, 136, 137, 138, 142, 146, 148, 153, 185
Diderot - - - 155

Diogenes - - - 32
Durand de Saint-Pourçain 87
Durokheim - - 74, 193

Empedocles - - - 5
Epictetus - - - 42
Epicurus 9, 35-39, 40, 125, 166, 182
Euhemerus - - - 34

Fénelon - - - 126
Fichte - - - 168, 169
Fontenelle - - - 126
Fouillée - - - - 193
Franklin - - - 16

Gassendi - - 125
Gerbert - - - - 70
Gerson - - - - 89
Gorgias - - 8, 11, 12, 31

Harvey - - - - 94
Havet (Ernest) - - 59
Hegel - - 170-178, 191
Hegesias - - - 34
Helvetius - - - 155
Heraclitus - - - 4, 20
Herillus - - - 42
Hermarchus - - - 38
Hobbes (Thomas) 100-104, 125, 145, 154, 155
Holbach (d') - - - 155
Horace - - - 33, 38, 39
Hugo (Victor) - - 141, 192
Hugo de Saint Victor - 77
Hume (David) 149-152, 154, 155, 157

Iamblichus - - - 50, 90
Izoulet - - - - 193

James I. - - - 97
Jesus Christ - 52, 53, 54, 56, 59
Joan of Navarre - - 88

Jouffroy - - - - 187
Justinian - - - 50

Kant 17, 146, 155, 157-169, 173, 191

La Bruyère - - - 30
Lamarck - - - 183
Lamennais - - - 188
Laromiguière - - - 185
Leibnitz 126, 136-141, 146, 157, 178
Leo X - - - - 91
Leucippus - - - 8
Liard - - - - 193
Locke - 126, 142-146, 152, 154
Louis XIV - - - 57
Lucian - - - - 32
Lucretius - - - 9, 38
Lulle (Raymond) - - 84

Maine de Biran 126, 185, 186
Malebranche 115, 126-129, 148, 193
Manes - - - - 56
Marcus Aurelius - - 42, 58
Menippus - - - 32
Metrodorus - - - 38
Moderatus - - - 44, 59
Molière - - - - 125
Montaigne - - - 16, 33
Moses - - - - 59, 60

Nemesius - - - 44, 59
Nero - - - - 58
Nicomachus - - - 44, 59
Nietzsche - 17, 180, 181, 194

Ockham (William of) - 87
Origen - - - - 60, 61

Paracelsus - - - 91
Parmenides - - 8, 10, 20
Pascal 11, 46, 83, 126, 134, 140

Paul (St.) - - - 51
Pericles - - - - 5
Philip the Fair - - 87
Philo - - - - 59
Pico della Mirandola - 90
Plato 11, 12, 19-28, 35, 36, 55, 59, 73, 78, 97, 166, 193
Pliny the Younger - - 38
Plotinus - - - 47-50
Plutarch- - - - 44
Poincaré (Henri) - - 46
Polemo - - - - 30
Polystratus - - - 38
Pomponazzo - - - 92-94
Porphyry - - - 50, 90
Prodicus - - - 11, 12
Protagoras - - - 11
Pyrrho - - - 44, 45
Pythagoras - - - 6, 20

Reid (Thomas) - 152, 185
Renan - - - 192, 193
Renouvier - - - 191
Reuchlin - - - 90
Ribot (Théodule) - - 193
Richard de Saint Victor - 77
Roscelin - - - 73
Rousseau (J.J.) 141, 154, 155, 185
Royer-Collard - - 185

Saisset (Emile) - - 188
Schelling - - 169, 170
Schopenhauer 96, 137, 178-180
Scotus Erigena - - 68, 69
Seneca - - - - 38, 42
Servetus (Michael) - - 94
Sextus Empiricus - - 46
Shakespeare - - - 97
Simon (Jules) - - - 188
Socrates 5, 8, 12, 14-18, 31, 33, 40, 45, 53
Spencer (Herbert) 183, 184, 191
Speusippus - - - 30
Spinoza - 126, 129-136, 151
Stewart (Dugald) - 152, 185

Taine (Hippolyte) - 191, 192
Thales - - - - 3
Theodosius - - - 56
Theophrastus - - 30
Thomas Aquinas (St.) - 78-83
Thrasea - - - 42
Timon - - - - 45

Vanini - - - 94
Vauvenargues - - 120
Vico - - - - 122
Villon - - - - 88
Vincent de Beauvais - 78
Voltaire - 33, 141, 145, 154

William d'Auvergne - 78
Wolf - - - - 157

Xenocrates - - - 30
Xenophanes - - - 7
Xenophon - - - 15, 19

Zeno (of Citium) 38, 40, 42, 166
Zeno (of Elea) - 8, 10, 31
Zoroaster - - - 6, 56

THE CROWN THEOLOGICAL LIBRARY.

In matters of religion the man of to-day is no longer satisfied with the statements which have been handed down to him about it from the past. He wants a religious literature which will deal with modern difficulties; he wants books which are really abreast of all that is best in modern research and thought.

The Crown Theological Library has been instituted to meet this pressing need. The volumes have all been selected with a view to answer the religious questionings of the present time, and each volume has been written by an acknowledged authority on the subject with which it deals.

The volumes are uniform in size (crown octavo) and binding, but the price varies according to the size and importance of the work.

Vol. I. **BABEL AND BIBLE.** By Dr. Friedrich Delitzsch, Professor of Assyriology in the University of Berlin. Authorised Translation. Edited, with an Introduction, by Rev. C. H. W. Johns Crown 8vo, with 77 illustrations, cloth. 4s. 6d. net.

Vol. II. **THE VIRGIN BIRTH OF CHRIST: An Historical and Critical Essay.** By Paul Lobstein, Professor of Dogmatics in the University of Strassburg. Edited, with an Introduction, by Rev. W. D. Morrison, LL.D. Crown 8vo. 2s. 6d. net.

Vol. III. **MY STRUGGLE FOR LIGHT: Confessions of a Preacher.** By R. Wimmer, Pastor of Weisweil-am-Rhein in Baden. Crown 8vo, cloth. 3s. net.

Vol. IV. **LIBERAL CHRISTIANITY: Its Origin, Nature, and Mission.** By Jean Réville, Professeur adjoint à la Faculté de Théologie Protestante de l'Université de Paris. Translated and edited by Victor Leuliette, A.K.C., B.-ès-L. Crown 8vo, cloth. 3s. 6d. net.

Vol. V. **WHAT IS CHRISTIANITY?** By Adolf Harnack, Professor of Church History in the University, Berlin. Translated by Thomas Bailey Saunders. Third and Revised Edition. Crown 8vo. 4s. 6d. net

Vol. VI. **FAITH AND MORALS.** By W. Herrmann, Professor of Systematic Theology at the University of Marburg; Author of "The Communion of the Christian with God." New Edition. Crown 8vo, cloth. 4s. 6d. net.

Vol. VII. **EARLY HEBREW STORY.** A Study of the Origin, the Value, and the Historical Background of the Legends of Israel. By John P. Peters, D.D., Rector of St. Michael's Church, New York. Crown 8vo, cloth. 4s. 6d. net.

Vol. VIII. **BIBLE PROBLEMS AND THE NEW MATERIAL FOR THEIR SOLUTION. A Plea for Thoroughness of Investigation addressed to Churchmen and Scholars.** By the Rev. T. K. Cheyne, D.Litt., D.D., Fellow of the British Academy. Crown 8vo. 4s. 6d. net.

Vol. IX. **THE DOCTRINE OF THE ATONEMENT AND ITS HISTORICAL EVOLUTION; and RELIGION AND MODERN CULTURE.** By the late Auguste Sabatier, Professor in the University of Paris. Translated by Victor Leuliette, A.K.C., B.-ès-L. Crown 8vo. 4s. net.

THE CROWN THEOLOGICAL LIBRARY—Continued.

Vol. X. **THE EARLY CHRISTIAN CONCEPTION OF CHRIST: Its value and Significance in the History of Religion.** By Otto Pfleiderer, D.D., Professor of Practical Theology in the University, Berlin. Crown 8vo. 3s. net.

Vol. XI. **THE CHILD AND RELIGION: Eleven Essays.** By Prof. Henry Jones, M.A., LL.D.; C. F. G. Masterman, M.A.; Prof. George T. Ladd, D.D., LL.D.; Rev. F. R. Tennant, M.A., B.Sc.; Rev. J. Cynddylan Jones, D.D.; Rev. Canon Hensley Henson, M.A.; Rev. Robert F. Horton, M.A., D.D.; Rev. G. Hill, M.A., D.D.; Rev. J. J. Thornton; Rev. Rabbi A. A. Green; Prof. Joseph Agar Beet, D.D. Edited by Thomas Stephens, B.A. Crown 8vo. 5s. net.

Vol. XII. **THE EVOLUTION OF RELIGION: an Anthropological Study.** By L. R. Farnell, D.Litt., Fellow and Tutor of Exeter College, Oxford; University Lecturer in Classical Archæology, etc., etc. Crown 8vo, cloth. 4s. 6d. net.

Vol. XIII. **THE BOOKS OF THE NEW TESTAMENT.** By H. Von Soden, D.D., Professor of Theology in the University of Berlin. Translated by the Rev. J. R. Wilkinson, and edited by Rev. W. D. Morrison, LL.D. Crown 8vo, cloth. 4s. 6d. net.

Vol. XIV. **JESUS.** By Wilhelm Bousset, Professor of Theology in Göttingen. Translated by Janet Penrose Trevelyan, and edited by Rev. W. D. Morrison, LL.D. Crown 8vo. 3s. 6d. net.

Vol. XV. **THE COMMUNION OF THE CHRISTIAN WITH GOD.** By Prof. Wilhelm Herrmann. Crown 8vo, cloth. 4s. 6d. net.

Vol. XVI. **HEBREW RELIGION TO THE ESTABLISHMENT OF JUDAISM UNDER EZRA.** By W. E. Addis, M.A. Crown 8vo. Cloth, 4s. 6d. net.

Vol. XVII. **NATURALISM AND RELIGION.** By Rudolf Otto, Professor of Theology in the University of Göttingen. Translated by Professor J. Arthur Thomson. Edited with an Introduction by Rev. W. D. Morrison, LL.D. Crown 8vo. 5s. net.

Vol. XVIII. **ESSAYS ON THE SOCIAL GOSPEL.** By Professor Adolf Harnack, of Berlin, and Professor W. Herrmann, of Marburg. Crown 8vo, cloth. 4s. net.

Vol. XIX. **THE RELIGION OF THE OLD TESTAMENT: Its Place among the Religions of the Nearer East.** By Karl Marti, Professor of Old Testament Exegesis, Bern. Crown 8vo, cloth. 4s. net.

Vol. XX. **LUKE, THE PHYSICIAN.** By Adolf Harnack, D.D. Translated by the Rev. J. R. Wilkinson, M.A. Being Vol. I. of Dr. Harnack's New Testament Studies. Crown 8vo, cloth. 5s. net.

Vol. XXI. **THE HISTORICAL EVIDENCE FOR THE RESURRECTION OF JESUS CHRIST.** By Kirsopp Lake, Professor of New Testament Exegesis in the University of Leiden, Holland. Crown 8vo, cloth. 4s. 6d. net.